THE LIBRARY
ST. MARY'S COLLEGE OF MARYLAND
ST. MARY'S CITY, MARYLAND 20686

AND THEY ALL SANG HALLELUJAH

And I'll sing, Hallelujah!

And you'll sing, Hallelujah!

And we'll all sing, Hallelujah!

When we arrive at home.

AND THEY ALL SANG HALLELUJAH

Plain-Folk Camp-Meeting Religion, 1800–1845

DICKSON D. BRUCE, JR.

The University of Tennessee Press

Knoxville

THIS BOOK
is the winner of the first
JAMES MOONEY AWARD (*1973*)
sponsored by the Southern Anthropological Society

Frontispiece:
Chorus from a camp-meeting spiritual.
William Hauser, *Hesperian Harp*, 102

COPYRIGHT © 1974 BY THE UNIVERSITY OF TENNESSEE PRESS, KNOXVILLE.
ALL RIGHTS RESERVED. MANUFACTURED IN THE UNITED STATES OF AMERICA.
FIRST EDITION.

Library of Congress Cataloging in Publication Data

Bruce, Dickson: D   1946-
    And they all sang hallelujah.

    Bibliography: p.
    1. Camp-meetings. 2. Southern States–Religion.
3. Frontier and pioneer life–United States–Southern
States. I. Title.
BV3798.B78   269'.2'0973   74–11344
ISBN 0–87049–157–1

FOR MARY

CONTENTS

ILLUSTRATIONS

ACKNOWLEDGMENTS

Oൢ NE RUNS UP HEAVY DEBTS writing a book; I owe much to the many people who have given me their encouragement and assistance. All those acknowledged here have played important roles in giving this study whatever value it may have.

The best single repository of tune books containing spiritual songs is the George Pullen Jackson Collection in the Department of Special Collections of the Library of the University of California, Los Angeles. Anyone who wishes to understand the life and religion of ante-bellum Southerners owes a special debt to the memory of Professor Jackson for his pioneer work on religious folksongs and the people who sang them, as well as for the care with which he collected and organized the material now in the collection bearing his name. The staff of the Department of Special Collections was most courteous and helpful to me during my research there. Funds from the United States Public Health Service Grant No. 5 R12 MH17216–02 provided partial support for my initial research in Los Angeles. This grant was administered by the Center for Urban Ethnography at the University of Pennsylvania, and I am grateful to the members of the Center for their assistance.

This study began as a doctoral dissertation in the Department of American Civilization at the University of Pennsylvania, under the direction of Robert M. Zemsky. He never failed to give incisive, if often troubling, criticism of everything I wrote. I only hope that by now I have answered most of his questions. The expertise in the areas of American religion, folklore and, particularly, religious folksong provided by Don Yoder was indispensable. John F. Szwed suggested many possible directions for this and future work.

I am very grateful to the Southern Anthropological Society for selecting the manuscript for the first James Mooney Award. Apart from the encouragement such an award provided, the comments of the members of the judging committee, chaired by Charles Hudson, were of great value. Samuel S. Hill, Jr., read the manuscript and made many important suggestions. Among my colleagues in the Program in Comparative Culture at the University of California, Irvine, Pete Clecak and James J. Flink read portions of the manuscript and prevented many mistakes. Dickran Tashjian deserves special mention. He read the entire manuscript at several stages of its development, and his comments were invariably clear and to the point. A lot of people gave me a lot of good advice: the mistakes which remain should not be assigned to them but to my own failure to pay close enough attention.

Had it not been for my wife Mary, I might never have done this study. In any case, she gave me far more support and assistance than I had any right to ask for.

AND THEY ALL SANG HALLELUJAH

INTRODUCTION

IN THE NINETEENTH-CENTURY ante-bellum South, the camp-meeting was a major social and religious institution. Southerners—black and white—often traveled great distances to take part in the annual religious gatherings, and crowds in the thousands might be in attendance at a meeting. They made for a stirring sight. As Timothy Flint, a traveler through the region, described the scene:

> The ambitious and wealthy are there, because in this region opinion is all powerful, and they are there either to extend their influence, or that their absence may not be noted, to diminish it. Aspirants for office are there, to electioneer and gain popularity. Vast numbers are there from simple curiosity, and merely to enjoy a spectacle. The young and beautiful are there, with mixed motives, which it were best not severely to scrutinize. Children are there, their young eyes glistening with the intense interest of eager curiosity.—The middle aged fathers and mothers of families are there, with the sober views of people, whose plans in life are fixed, and calmly waiting to hear. Men and women of hoary hairs are there, with such tho'ts it may be hoped, as their years invite.—Such is the congregation consisting of thousands . . . .[1]

[1] "From Flint's work on the Geography and History of the Western States, just published," quoted in the Huntsville, Ala., *Southern Advocate*, Oct. 10, 1828.

Still, although camp-meetings attracted all sorts of people for a variety of reasons—religious and otherwise—for most who took the exercises seriously, "singing hallelujah" was a major part of what the gathering was about.

For all its social importance, the camp-meeting was first and foremost a religious activity. The religion it conveyed was a remarkable synthesis, born in the South, of elements from several branches of European Protestantism in combination with values and practices unique to the Southern frontier. Aimed at converting the population from irreligion to the church, camp-meeting religion offered not only a coherent view of man's place in the world, but also a way of handling the difficulties of life on the frontier.

One tends to think of the Southern United States both as profoundly religious and as dominated by the Methodist and Baptist versions of Christianity, but such was not always the case. At the opening of the nineteenth century, members of both denominations were definitely a minority of the Southern population, as were religious people generally. Indeed, in many parts of the South the two churches faced hostility and even persecution from the irreligious majority. Nevertheless, although they never reached majority status during the ante-bellum period, the two denominations were able to convert a substantial number of people, largely by means of the camp-meeting, and came to occupy a place of some influence in Southern society.

Part of the reason for the measure of success that both Methodists and Baptists achieved lay in their aiming the thrust of their evangelistic efforts toward that part of the Southern population which has come to be known as the "plain-folk."[2] Comprising the

---

[2] The term "plain-folk" has become, after Frank Lawrence Owsley, the technical term for referring to the great mass of ante-bellum Southern farmers and townspeople who were neither rich nor starving, and it is used in that technical sense here. See Owsley, *Plain Folk of the Old South*. Others, including Blanche H. Clark, have used the term "yeomen" or, as in the case of Ulrich B. Phillips and Bell Irvin Wiley, have chosen to call this group "the plain people." The former term carries possibly intrusive ideological connotations, while the latter has more traditionally been used to describe certain "plain dress" religious sectarians and could be particularly confusing in the context of this study.

greatest number of ante-bellum Southerners, these small farmers and townspeople were truly the forgotten people of the Old South, and their lives have remained of secondary importance to historians, with but few exceptions. The Southern economy was geared to plantation agriculture for export, whereas the plain-folk engaged primarily in subsistence farming and thus were marginal to the major political, economic, and social considerations of the ante-bellum South.

They were, nonetheless, objects of a great deal of interest to early Baptist and Methodist evangelists. Although both churches were active among the slaves and would have a fair representation among the elite by the time of the Civil War, Baptists and Methodists alike made their strongest appeals to the white plain-folk. Moreover, such people provided the churches' most energetic leadership since most preachers came from plain-folk families. Over time, then, as religion adjusted its practices to cope with the frontier environment and its teachings to reach a frontier audience, the plain-folk came more and more to put their own distinctive stamp upon Methodist and Baptist traditions. Where the churches took stands on social issues, their stands often reflected plain-folk interests. More than that, where there had been theological differences separating the two denominations, such differences disappeared on the frontier as both denominations parted in significant ways from the older European traditions. Aimed toward plain-folk and led by plain-folk, camp-meeting religion can be called without exaggeration a creation of the plain-folk.

At the same time, it should be noted that what the plain-folk created was indeed a religion. So much has been made of the camp-meeting's frontier origins as well as of its more sensational qualities that one often loses sight of its religious character and the content of its religious appeal. For many observers, then and now, the secular social role of the camp-meeting has far overshadowed whatever religious significance the practice might have had. Recognizing the hard character of frontier life, these writers have shown that the plain-folk greatly needed the kind of social occasion afforded by camp-meetings. Gatherings provided an opportunity, usually right after harvest time, for people to get together for several days of unencumbered social activity, and in a region where population was sparse and work hard, such an opportunity must have been greatly appreciated.

Moreover, a number of historians have also seen a tie between secular Southern beliefs and values and the religious activities of frontier religion. Focusing on the individualism of the camp-meeting's message of salvation, as well as on the egalitarianism and anti-intellectualism of the revival movement, many writers have tried to account for the success of the practice by pointing out its coherence with values and ideas that were present in Southern life anyway.[3] Such a coherence undoubtedly existed, and the content of secular beliefs almost certainly helped to determine the sort of religion plain-folk would create.

Frontier life may have had something to do, as well, with the rather sensational forms of conversion which occurred. Camp-meeting conversions were frequently accompanied by enthusiastic physical and emotional displays which have been accounted for in a variety of ways. In terms of religion, it has been suggested that such displays indicated the degree to which emotion dominated belief among the plain-folk. More than that, many writers, noting again the brutal realities of frontier life, have seen the emotional extravagances of the camp-meeting as a device by means of which frontier folk could let off all the tensions which must have built up in a year's time.[4] Frontier life did have profound effects on plain-folk to which religion was certainly forced to respond, and the sensational quality of religious experience was surely influenced by the harshness of that life.

Approaching the camp-meeting as a social institution with clear ties to plain-folk on the frontier illuminates both the nature of the practice and the character of plain-folk communities. Moreover, such an approach highlights the unique quality of camp-meeting religion and points clearly to the fact that in both belief and prac-

---

[3] Such seems to be the view taken by, for example, Arthur K. Moore in *The Frontier Mind*, 229–37.

[4] See, for example, George Rosen, *Madness in Society*, 217. For an earlier statement of this view, see Catharine C. Cleveland, *The Great Revival in the West, 1797–1805*, 120–21.

tice it was something quite different from its European antecedents. At the same time, a social interpretation takes into account that, like any religion, that of the camp-meeting would have had small success had it not answered the special needs of its believers. Where such an exclusively social view falls short, however, is in its failure to take the explicitly religious content of the camp-meeting as seriously as it might, for it tends to lead one to characterize the camp-meeting as merely a social event with a religious veneer. While pointing to the emotional quality of the camp-meeting, this approach often leads one to neglect to specify what religious symbols made the emotional appeals work. Noting the sensational quality of conversion, those who focus on the social importance of the meeting often fail to make clear what one was converted from or to. Yet such questions were crucial to frontier believers.

This is not to say that the religious aspects of the camp-meeting have been ignored. Church historians and theologians from within and outside the camp-meeting denominations have discussed at length the place of the device within church traditions and the concerns which leaders of various persuasions had about the practice. No denomination ever displayed any unanimity of feeling about the camp-meeting, and in no group was the practice made official. As a very early historian of American Methodism, Jesse Lee, described the situation:

> Indeed, these meetings have never been authorized by the Methodists, either at their general or annual conferences. They have been allowed of; but we, as a body of people, have never made any rules or regulations about them; we allow our presiding elders and travelling preachers to appoint them when and where they please, and to conduct them in what manner they think fit.[5]

Lee acknowledged here not only the plain-folk's role in the development of camp-meeting practices, but also the unwillingness of the general body of Methodists to grant their approval. Methodist journals frequently contained articles claiming the merit or the lack of merit of religion on the campground—its partisans

[5] Jesse Lee, *A Short History of the Methodists*, 367.

proclaiming the conversions of thousands, its detractors wondering what those conversions were worth. And the Methodists were the most hospitable denomination. Among Baptists and Presbyterians even the process of evangelism, with its implied Arminianism, was open to question. Such denominational and theological issues dogged the camp-meeting from its inception, and the resulting discussions have provided a great deal of information about camp-meeting practice.

The writings of church leaders can provide excellent sources for constructing an intellectual history of the camp-meeting. Though most ministers and other religious functionaries were of plain-folk background, their professional status gave them opportunities which set them apart from their congregations. If the Methodists, especially, were often hostile to the formal education of ministers, they encouraged self-education so that most Methodist preachers were not unread. One might well expect the preachers to have carried a Bible, a hymn book, and the Methodist Discipline, but it was not unusual for the preachers' saddlebags to contain as well the writings of John Wesley, Thomas à Kempis, and Richard Baxter's *Saints Everlasting Rest*, all of which "furnished the armory from whence the itinerants of those days drew the weapons of their spiritual warfare."[6] As a result, when church leaders wrote about the camp-meeting, positively or negatively, they tended to frame their discussions in terms closer to their traditional Protestant heritage than to the frontier on which the practice was born. An intellectual history of the revival movement is necessary, but it tells only part of the story of the camp-meeting's success.[7]

What of most of those who "found salvation" at the camp-meeting? What, first of all, was the nature of the salvation which they found, or how, at least, did they conceive it? Further, how did their conceptions of camp-meeting religion relate to their lives as plain-folk and as Southerners? Even to approach these questions,

6 William P. Strickland, *The Life of Jacob Gruber*, 30.

7 For a good survey of the views of the camp-meeting's contemporaries, as well as of the views of historians up to the 1950s, see Charles A. Johnson, "The Frontier Camp-Meeting: Contemporary and Historical Appraisals," *Mississippi Valley Historical Review* 37 (1950–51), 91–110.

one must attempt to understand camp-meeting religion as a coherent system of belief, religious in content but distinct from its European intellectual heritage, with a life of its own. This study seeks to arrive at such an understanding.

In attempting to describe the main features of camp-meetings, one must seek, above all, to understand the plain-folk's religious activities and expressions on their own terms.[8] Doing so involves, on the one hand, explicating plain-folk religious symbolism as the plain-folk themselves might have done, rather than simply taking the religious terms they used to mean about the same as those terms have always meant. Plain-folk religious expression was, in fact, remarkably coherent, and by noting the consistencies in their activities and statements of belief as well as the constant patterns which appear to have been at the base of the overall body of expression, one can set forth frontier beliefs in systematic form. In addition, understanding plain-folk religion on its own terms means that before one can try to account for that religion, one must first try to see how such things as the camp-meeting were related to what the plain-folk themselves took to be their ultimate goals in religion, namely, conversion and salvation. No analysis can proceed, in other words, without some prior sense of what the people themselves intended to be about.

Since much of the historical debate over the camp-meeting has focused on its more sensational events, many observers have failed to note that the meetings consisted of more than dawn-to-dusk shouting. Instead, each camp-meeting day appears to have been rigorously planned to include several kinds of services at regular intervals, and, further, the activities within each of the kinds of services were fairly standardized from meeting to meeting.

These patterns may be described on the basis of a variety of sources. Many of those who participated in camp-meetings have left their own accounts of what the meetings were like and of how the meetings affected their lives and the lives of their friends; in addition, some revival leaders wrote camp-meeting manuals to

[8] Here, I am drawing most explicitly on Anthony F. C. Wallace, *Religion: An Anthropological View*, 107.

9

give guidelines for others to follow in order to achieve success. Such accounts and manuals by friends of the practice contain a rather complete picture of those elements which were a constant part of camp-meeting activities. Further, few travelers through the Old South did not try to put a camp-meeting on their itineraries. Though these outsiders had differing views on the practice—some were quite sympathetic; others, unwaveringly hostile—they nevertheless gave very similar descriptions of what they had seen. From such sources, then, it is possible to reconstruct that pattern of events which appears to have constituted the basis for most camp-meetings.

The structure of such a ritual as the camp-meeting has symbolic as well as social importance. Not only do the organizational patterns of a ritual dictate how participants are to act, but the structure is also founded in the ideas which participants accept with regard to their own relationships to each other and to the divine. The structure supporting camp-meetings may be seen as a norm for plain-folk religious behavior, and its correct observation was directly related to the accomplishment of the camp-meeting's major goal of conversion. A major part of the analysis of camp-meeting religion, then, lies in the delineation of the normative structure of ritual behavior and in tracing the connection between that structure and the goal of the meeting.

But a study of the camp-meeting in itself leads one to ask further how the plain-folk interpreted what they were doing, and to look, therefore, for expressions of their views in their own words. In part, plain-folk exegesis can be derived from the writings of ministers and other leaders, especially from their autobiographies, but, again, although such men could set the prevailing ideological tone, one may well question the extent to which their accounts were colored by their status. One must try to examine as well the words of members of the congregations, and indeed the plain-folk further did develop a significant body of expression which was created right on the campground in the form of camp-meeting spiritual songs. Written down by singing-school teachers, these songs, grew out of the demands of the frontier environment on religion, for they were both rousing and easily sung.

Anyone who wanted to participate in a camp-meeting could also join in singing the simple, repeated words of the songs. Because of their breadth of content and their close ties to the camp-meeting and its participants, the spiritual songs may well be the best indicators of the ways in which most religious plain-folk interpreted what the camp-meeting was about.

An understanding of camp-meeting religion thus comes from the things which plain-folk themselves said and did with regard to religious belief. What results from the study is an account of that coherent system of religious symbols which was unique to the plain-folk of the Old South. The symbol system differed in significant ways from Old World religious traditions, combining ideas from several different groups along with attitudes unique to the South.[9] Moreover, even if much of both practice and belief had a great deal to do with secular values and frontier conditions, camp-meeting symbolism had a profound religious integrity that set it off from other aspects of Southern social life.

Yet, a delineation of plain-folk religious belief would be little more than an exercise if, from it, one could learn nothing new about the believers themselves. One must go beyond the question of what plain-folk believed and ask, as well, why they might have believed as they did. If camp-meeting religion is seen as a system of religious symbols inextricably bound to the people of the frontier, it then becomes possible to approach the latter question. Though there are many ways to view what religion does in a community, the system of symbols which comprise a religion may be taken as a construct which, above all, gives some degree of order to people's lives and to the world in which they live. A religious system, in other words, is a set of attitudes and actions which enables its adherents to know who they are and how they are to consider others, and hence allows those who believe some basis on which to deal with the events of the world.[10] When people on the

[9] A good discussion of the sources of Southern belief may be found in Samuel S. Hill, Jr., *Southern Churches in Crisis*, ch. 8.

[10] My view of the relation of religion to society has been greatly influenced by the work of Robin Horton; see especially "African Conversion," *Africa* 41 (1971), 94, and "The Kalibari World View: An Outline and Interpretation,"

Southern frontier were converted to religion, they were brought to look at themselves and their world in a certain way. From an understanding of how they came to see the world in religious terms, one can also derive a picture of the nature of Southern life and the plain-folk's notions of their place in it. The study of camp-meeting religion has, then, a much broader purpose: a delineation of the world-view of a significant number of ante-bellum Southerners.

This study begins with the context in which camp-meeting religion grew up and flowered: first, with a description of plain-folk life and an interpretation of their place in the Southern world; second, with an account of the Methodist and Baptist churches as Southern institutions and of the camp-meeting as a practice. Once the context of camp-meeting religion has been described, it then becomes possible to set out the contents of the plain-folk religious belief system. To do this, there is an examination of the structure and content of the camp-meeting and its relationship to the central purpose of Southern evangelical religion, conversion. Then the study turns to the spiritual songs in order to outline what most of those who were converted proclaimed their salvation to mean. Finally, the study comes full circle to examine again the plain-folk and their lives, but at that point to see what camp-meeting religion did for those who gave themselves over to it.

Africa 32 (1962), passim. See also Murray G. Murphey, "On the Relation between Science and Religion," *American Quarterly* 20 (1968), 275–95.

THE WILDERNESS BELOW

Life on the Southern Frontier

THE PEOPLE of the Old South have been called a people of the frontier; their history, that of a constantly moving frontier society. Although these descriptions are only partly true for the large planters and the slaves, a sizable number of Southern whites did lead frontier lives, and much of what has seemed unique about the ante-bellum white Southerner—his social life, his folkways, and even the kind of man he aspired to be—can be attributed to frontier influences. Above all, the frontier environment contributed to the founding of the Methodist and Baptist sects, religious bodies which have grown into the great Southern churches of our own time.

Methodists and Baptists were present in the South during the colonial period, but the two organizations did not begin to gather real strength until after about 1800. As Southern whites moved from old lands to new, missionaries of the two denominations moved along with them, conducting revivals, bringing souls to God, and founding churches. It was a cycle which would continue up to the time of the Civil War.

The practices and teachings of these religious organizations, and whatever success their representatives had in reaching people, can best be understood in the context of the frontier setting. Although the teachings of the missionaries have been considered otherworldly and escapist, and the revival methods employed have been viewed as, at best, harmless recreation or, at worst, symptoms of a frontier regression to barbarism, the Methodists and Baptists answered some very real problems for frontier farm families. Such problems arose from conflicts that, in large measure, were produced by the social and physical environment.

The Southern "frontier" was a condition rather than a particular geographical area. It was not simply that Southerners, like many other white Americans, were moving west, changing the continent into a land of farms, but rather that even the lands behind the line of European settlement in the South contained few established, stable communities. They remained sparsely populated regions, inhabited by people who never stayed in one place for a very long period of time—a perpetual frontier maintained by the continual quest of large numbers of white Southern farmers for new land.

From colonial times to the coming of the Civil War, the opening of each new territory for settlement created a dramatic influx of land-hungry people. As the backcountry was opened up in the eighteenth century, settlers poured in from the North and Europe, as well as from the nearby Tidewater South. Scotch-Irish Presbyterians and Germans immigrated via Pennsylvania, while Englishmen and many German sectarians entered directly from the Old World. As these diverse peoples mingled, however, and as European and Northern immigration dropped sharply with relation to the total number of migrants, ethnic lines began to blur and then to disappear. It was not long before the bulk of settlers in any new territory could only be called "Southerners."

New territories grew rapidly, from the opening of Kentucky in the late eighteenth century to the colonization of the lower South and Texas in the following century. The first permanent settlement of Kentucky began about 1775 with the founding of Boonesborough and Harrodsburg, and by 1790 the population had reached nearly 74,000. During the next decade, the state would experience a population increase of some 200 percent. The case of Tennessee was just as spectacular, the high rate of growth being maintained until about 1830. When the territories of the lower South became available for permanent settlement in 1798, the rush for land was even greater than that into Kentucky and Tennessee. By 1810 more than 40,000 people occupied the Mississippi Territory, embracing the present states of Alabama and Mississippi, and during the next ten years the population of Alabama alone increased over 1,000 percent, while that of Mississippi more than doubled. By the time of the Civil War, each of these states exceeded in population the older Southern state of South Carolina.[1]

It is not sufficient, however, to characterize Southern migration as merely an ongoing westward movement. In the Mississippi Territory, for instance, the settlement movement was not continuous, but occurred in three separate waves from 1798 on into the 1830s.[2] The first wave lasted from the opening of the territory until the coming of the War of 1812; the second extended from the end of the war to the financial panic of 1819; and the third, in the 1830s, occurred at a time when the older Southern states were experiencing difficulties while the Alabama and Mississippi regions enjoyed apparent prosperity plus vast quantities of land made newly available by the forced removal of the Indians.[3] People appear to have migrated to the lower South in search of good cheap land, embarking on their quest when prospects for success appeared good, and what was true for the Mississippi Territory was true for the rest of the South as well.

The leaders of this Southern migration, aside from the herdsmen and squatters who showed little interest in the permanent acquisition of land, were the small farmers, often called the Southern "plain-folk," who owned no slaves, or at most a few. Planters and large slaveholders represented no more than a small fraction of the migrating population. For instance, slaves constituted only about 10 to 20 percent of the first settlers in Kentucky and Tennessee; while their proportion among the first settlers of the lower South was substantially larger, it is still clear that most of the white immigrants brought few slaves or none with them. Only

---

[1] U. S. Dept. of Commerce, Bureau of the Census, *The Statistical History of the United States from Colonial Times to the Present,* 13.

[2] Ibid. See also Charles D. Lowery, "The Great Migration to the Mississippi Territory, 1789–1819," *Journal of Mississippi History* 30 (1968), 185.

[3] Charles S. Sydnor, *The Development of Southern Sectionalism, 1819–1848,* 255.

in later years, after the groundwork of permanent agricultural society had been laid, would the planters begin to move into new territories.[4] Thus, the first settlers to move into the territory were the plain-folk, and though migration would become something of a slaveowners' movement in subsequent years, the clear tendency for small farmers to change place of residence more frequently than planters would remain unchanged.[5]

Unfortunately, statistics fail to reveal the extent of movement *within* the South, although demographers have long recognized that the Southern population was extraordinarily mobile behind the line of settlement and, hence, that the Southern frontier was something more than the western limit of settlement. Individual case histories, such as that of Gideon Linecum, tell far more than census figures ever could. Linecum was born in Georgia in 1793, soon after his father's family had moved there from North Carolina. In 1802 the family sold its farm and moved to South Carolina. Shortly thereafter the Linecums went to Athens, Georgia, but in 1805 returned to South Carolina. A year later the family was back in Georgia, about a mile from the earlier home; then, after a short time, the Linecums moved again, this time to the lower South. By

---

[4] U. S. Dept. of Commerce, Bureau of the Census, *Negro Population, 1790–1915*, 45, 51. The extent of slaveholdings which made one a planter depended, of course, upon what one was trying to produce for market. Tobacco was grown most efficiently on small plantations, while sugar required a large number of workers. In general, however, one may accept Phillips' statement that holdings of twenty or fewer slaves "were too small for the full plantation order." Ulrich B. Phillips, *Life and Labor in the Old South*, 207. Given the small percentage of blacks among early settlers, then, it is unlikely that many planters were among the migrants.

[5] Fabian Linden has shown that there was some correlation between the extent of slaveholdings and the tendency to migrate, at least in the decade 1840–50. Census figures will not permit one to say much about the years before that decade. Some 86.9 percent of nonslaveholders changed residence between 1840 and 1850; 81.1 percent of those who held two to nine slaves; 76.1 percent of those holding ten to forty-nine slaves; 50.9 percent of those with fifty to ninety-nine slaves; and only 16.7 percent of those with over one hundred slaves. In part, the differences may have been due to the difficulties involved in moving a large plantation, but the figures do show that plain-folk were more mobile than planters. See Linden, "Economic Democracy in the Slave South: An Appraisal of Some Recent Views," *Journal of Negro History* 31 (1946), 175.

now Gideon had come of age and, with his father, moved to a farm on the Ocmulgee River in Georgia. Two or three years later he and his father, in the company of others, were off again, first to the area around Tuscaloosa, Alabama, and next "to the Tombigby River" near Columbus, Mississippi. He seems to have remained there for a while before finally moving on to Texas in the 1840s.[6]

The life of William Physick Zuber, another native Georgian, was similar to that of Linecum. Zuber's mother had been born in South Carolina, moving to Georgia in 1815, and his father, a Pennsylvania native who had migrated with his parents to Georgia in 1786, had settled in Twiggs County shortly before William was born there in 1820. When William was two years old, the family departed Georgia for Montgomery County (now Lowndes County), Alabama, where the Zubers remained for another two years. Next they located in East Feliciana Parish, Louisiana. Two years later, in 1826, the family moved to St. Helena Parish, stayed there four years, and then joined Austin's colony to settle in Texas. In 1833 the Zubers relocated in Grimes County, Texas. There they resided for the longest period yet, a total of six years.[7]

The wanderings of Gideon Linecum and William Physick Zuber were of course duplicated by countless other Southerners behind the pioneer line of settlement. If the white Southerner was not himself moving, he was surely conscious of, and affected by, the transitory nature of his friends and neighbors, as well as by the migrants joining him from other regions. All factors would tend to delay stability and prolong frontier conditions. Of more importance, however, is the question of why these Southerners were so mobile: what was the cause of their continual movement, especially within the region? The explanation that frontiersmen had "a repugnance to permanent homes until they had moved several times,"[8] while having some validity, may identify a symptom

---

[6] "Autobiography of Gideon Linecum," in *Plantation and Frontier, 1649–1863*, ed. Ulrich B. Phillips, 2 vols., II, 185–96.

[7] William Physick Zuber, *My Eighty Years in Texas*, ed. Janis Boyle Mayfield, 12–36.

[8] Carl Bridenbaugh, *Myths and Realities*, 132. Thomas Perkins Abernethy

rather than a cause. Instead, the characteristics of migration indicate that a more significant reason for plain-folk mobility must have been their place within the Southern political economy, for it was an insecure place, almost that of an outsider.

Owning no slaves or only a few, these small farmers were never important to the staple crop economy of the ante-bellum period. Although they did grow some cash crops in order to purchase luxury items and staples, the plain-folk concentrated on subsistence, balanced agriculture, producing corn, oats, wheat, and black-eyed peas, and raising cattle and hogs. At no time prior to the Civil War did nonslaveholders produce more than 7 percent of the big money crop cotton in Mississippi, and they never grew more than 5 percent of the tobacco in Virginia. Hemp, a mainstay of the Kentucky economy, was regarded by plain-folk as a "nigger-crop."[9] Although constituting the bulk of the ante-bellum Southern population, the farmers occupied a marginal position in the Southern economy, a position reflected in the distribution of income just prior to the Civil War. The 3,000 to 4,000 families on the best lands received about three-quarters of the total returns from Southern exports; indeed, in 1860 the 1,000 most prosperous families received over fifty million dollars a year, while the remaining 660,000 families received only about sixty million.[10]

Economic marginality was accompanied by political marginality, especially before 1850. Legislative representation in several states was based either on total population—including the slaves —or on the federal ratio, both plans favoring those districts in which plantations rather than farms predominated. As one farmer told a Northerner traveling in the South:

"Why you see, they vote on the slave basis, and there's some of them nigger counties where there ain't more'n four or five hundred white folks, that has just as much power in the Legislature

has described many of the early settlers in Kentucky as "aimless drifters" in *Three Virginia Frontiers*, 65.

9 Clement Eaton, *The Growth of Southern Civilization, 1790–1860*, 156.
10 Rupert B. Vance, *Human Factors in Cotton Culture*, 44.

as any of our mountain counties where there'll be some thousand voters."[11]

The planters, furthermore, used their domination to maintain their hegemony: in the formative years of each Southern state they were able to establish slavery and to ensure, through suffrage requirements, their continued power; subsequently they made sure that taxes on their slave "properties" would remain light.

For all this, the possibility of advancing himself socially and economically was not closed to the Southern white farmer. The classes were by no means constant in personnel, even though inherited wealth generally brought continued comfort and inherited poverty was hard to overcome.[12] In the lower South, as in Tennessee and Kentucky, most of the professional people came from outside the planter class,[13] as did many political leaders and even some of those involved in proslavery movements. W. J. Cash vividly described the rise of "a stout young Irishman" from backwoods pioneer to Charleston legislator who could leave a legacy of "two thousand acres, a hundred and fourteen slaves, and four cotton gins," and such a career plan was no doubt followed by many ambitious white Southerners.[14]

Consequently, even though the small farmer occupied a marginal position within the South, he had reason to believe in the possibility of his upward movement within the system. This probably was the reason that, despite his sometimes bitter resentment of the planters' authority, he rarely undertook to challenge the Southern system and its leaders.[15] In 1849 a group of nonslaveholders tried to abolish slavery in Kentucky, but the voters, seven-

[11] Frederick Law Olmsted, *A Journey in the Back Country*, 259–60.

[12] Phillips, *Life and Labor*, 346.

[13] Owsley, *Plain Folk*, 142–43.

[14] W. J. Cash, *The Mind of the South*, 14–17. An example of such a career would be that of Gideon Linecum; Phillips, ed., *Plantation and Frontier*, II, 185.

[15] Plain-folk bitterness showed up in the diatribes of Hinton Rowan Helper, who was hardly typical, or in the words of a farmer quoted by Olmsted who described the planters as "aristocrats" and "swellheads," in *Journey in the Back Country*, 25.

MAP 1. The travels of Gideon Linecum (1802 to 1818, from S. C. to Miss.) and William Physick Zuber (1820 to 1833, from Ga. to Tex.) are typical of migration by plain-folk within the South.

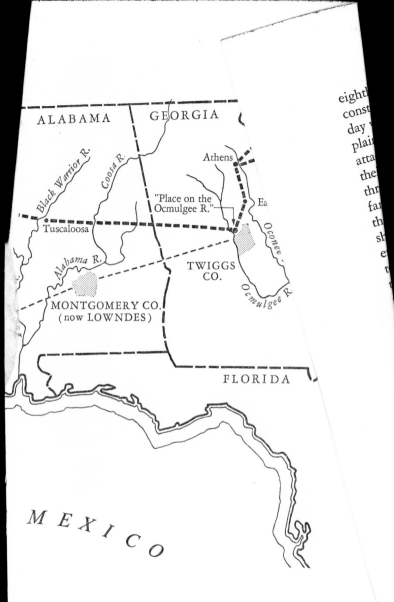

s of whom held no slaves, approved by a wide margin ɩ tutional amendment to *protect* the institution.[16] The day-to-ork of patrolling for runaway slaves was undertaken by the -folk. Nonslaveholders also participated actively in Southern ks on abolitionism, often, perhaps, outdoing the planters in r defense of slavery; and when the system received its ultimate at, the Confederacy could draw largely on nonslaveholding ilies for her fighting forces.[17] The plain-folk were devoted to Southern way of life, and whereas the importance of racism ould not be slighted—the farmers may have resented the plant-s, but they actually hated and feared the blacks—their failure challenge the plantation system may also have stemmed from heir belief that, given enough breaks and with a lot of hard work, hey too could rise into the elite.

The plain-folk's marginal status in the Southern system, working against a hope for an improved position, accounted for much of the internal migration in the Old South. Again, small farmers led the migrations, and the movements were particularly heavy when times were good. The migrants were not "aimless drifters." Rather, they were people who thought that by leaving their old farms and starting afresh in a new territory they could achieve a measure of success and security.

Some succeeded; most, of course, did not. Their failure was ensured by their inability to acquire and hold good land adequately served by transportation. The great majority of plain-folk lived outside the principal staple-crop growing districts, on land that was inaccessible to markets, while the planters dominated the good lands along rivers and roads. The South may have been a frontier, but it was never a poor man's frontier.[18] Although the farmers arrived in new regions first, the best lands had already been bought

[16] Eaton, *Growth*, 176.

[17] For the role of nonslaveholders in proslavery movements, see Sydnor, *Development of Southern Sectionalism*, 290, and Ronald T. Takaki, *A Pro-Slavery Crusade*, 21, 58. For the role of the plain-folk in the Civil War, see Bell Irvin Wiley, *The Plain People of the Confederacy*, chs. 1–2.

[18] Abernethy specifically says this of Kentucky in *Three Virginia Frontiers*, 65.

up by planter speculators. The rich bluegrass region of Kentucky was dominated by the Virginia elite by 1795, and planter-controlled land companies had received grants to areas of the lower South as early as 1783, some twelve years before the United States gained undisputed title to the region.[19] Further, when the government put new tracts of land up for sale, speculators came to the auctions to bid against the small farmer, running the price well beyond the farmer's ability to pay. When the plain-folk were not cooperative with the speculators, the land hunters were not above extortion, nor would they hesitate to badger the settler until, as with Gideon Linecum, his money was "eaten up."[20] In cases where the government did grant preemption rights, usually on the less desirable lands, the minimum price was still far beyond the means of most farmers.[21] Accordingly, when the plantation economy developed in an area, the farmers moved out in what was to become a continual migration to escape planter encroachment.

Crowded off the best lands, plain-folk tended to be congregated in particular neighborhoods, even though they lived throughout the South. In the Alabama black belt some 40 percent of the whites were nonslaveholders,[22] but they did not live side by side with the planters, as illustrated by the situation of Wade Hampton Richardson, a black-belt farmer. Born in Georgia in 1847, Richardson was taken by his family to Chambers County, Alabama, and from there to Macon County, in the black belt, where he remained until the Civil War. His family owned a five-hundred-acre farm on which were grown corn and grains. Although living in a black-belt county, the nonslaveholding Richardson did not occupy the fertile lowlands where slaves worked the crops, but owned instead a farm on the poorer uplands. In his own neighborhood the population was 90 percent white, but he could go only about five miles to the south to find a population of roughly 90 percent black slaves. "Thus it was throughout the South," he wrote; "the more fertile lands were given up to cotton raising, hence was

[19] Ibid.; see also Abernethy, *The South in the New Nation, 1789–1819*, 75.
[20] In Phillips, ed., *Plantation and Frontier*, II, 194.
[21] Abernethy, *South in the New Nation*, 453.
[22] Eaton, *Growth*, 158.

gradually acquired by the slaveowners."[23] Frederick Law Olmsted observed the same pattern in his journey through the interior cotton districts: where the soil was rich, plantations predominated, and the white population was extremely small. Those whites who were not plantation owners occupied smaller farms on less valuable lands.[24]

The small farms and domestic economy of these plain-folk therefore came to dominate certain upland areas of the South—the uplands and highlands of middle and western North Carolina, poorer lands in the Valley of Virginia, the northern parts of Georgia and Alabama, the foothills and mountains of Tennessee and Kentucky, and the mountainous regions of west Virginia. Seldom remaining in one place permanently, the plain-folk migrated to other upland areas or even to the North,[25] ever hoping to better their lot. As writers from Olmsted to Cash have remarked, the Old South remained a frontier up to the time of the Civil War, and this continual movement was a major force in making it so.

In such a frontier environment the farmer's way of life was difficult. He liked to think of himself as strong and self-reliant, the equal of any man, and in full control of his own destiny; yet, the fact was that, if compelled to depend solely on his own re-

[23] From sections of Richardson's memoirs in "Rural Life in Ante-Bellum Alabama," ed. Walter F. Peterson, *Alabama Review* 19 (1966), 138–39.

[24] Olmsted, *Journey in the Back Country*, 197–98. The extent to which the planters dominated the good lands is reflected in the patterns of land ownership in the rich farming areas. In 1850 approximately 64 percent of all black-belt acres were held by about 17 percent of the population as part of plantations of 500 acres or more. Slaveholders, regardless of the extent of their holdings, accounted for 56 percent of the farming families in the black belt, but controlled 88 percent of the land (Linden, "Economic Democracy," table I, p. 150). Similarly, in the rich county of Bolivar, Mississippi, planters who held twenty or more slaves, about 58 percent of the landowners, held 69 percent of the land, and the average value of their plantations—not, apparently, including slaves—was almost two and one-half times that of the small farms (computations based on figures in Owsley, *Plain Folk*, table III, p. 15).

[25] Rupert B. Vance, *Human Geography of the South*, 44. See also Solon J. Buck and Elizabeth Hawthorn Buck, *The Planting of Civilization in Western Pennsylvania*, 151; and Solon Justus Buck, *Illinois in 1818*, 2nd ed., rev., 94–95 for the role of Southerners in the settlement of Northern border states.

sources, he was unlikely to succeed or even to survive on the Southern frontier. He could not compete against the planters for good lands or political power, and even within his own neighborhood he was forced to rely on a relationship of mutual dependence with his neighbors in order to exist.

The settlement of the South from colonial times on was achieved by families rather than by isolated individuals. Moreover, the domestic subsistence agriculture of the frontier farm was based upon the family as an index of both need and capacity. Although the plain-folk might move to new lands in groups which were based on kinship, so that several generations would be present in a body of migrants—as, for example, Gideon Linecum traveled with his family even after coming of age—when they reached their new home, the group usually broke up, and each household tried to start a farm all its own. Every household member—father, mother, and children—then had to participate in the growing of crops.[26] Still, there were some jobs which were too great for a lone family to undertake. Even when the farmer was a slaveholder, his holdings were too small for the slaves to provide anything more than assistance in farm work. For the major tasks of frontier life, a "principle of mutuality"[27] operated to bring out the whole neighborhood.

Cooperative effort began with the reception of a new neighbor. The experience of a man who settled in Illinois in 1817 was duplicated throughout the South:

> When a new-comer arrived in the country, the settlers, without distinction or ceremony, went at once to pay him a visit, whom they found in a tent or camp. The warmest sentiments of friendship and good-will were interchanged, the old settlers assuring the new neighbor, that every thing they possessed, in the way of tools, teams, wagons, provisions, and their own personal services, were entirely at his command. Hence, in a few days, all hands, as the phrase then was, turned out, and built the new-

[26] Bridenbaugh, *Myths and Realities*, 135; Vance, *Human Geography*, 67.
[27] Mody C. Boatright, "The Myth of Frontier Individualism," in *Turner and the Sociology of the Frontier*, ed. Richard Hofstadter and Seymour Martin Lipset, 45.

comer a house, cut and split his rails, hauled them out, put them up in fence around the land he wished to cultivate, and then his land was broken up for him ready to seed. Thus, in the space of a few days, the new-comer was in a comfortable condition, well-acquainted and upon the best terms of friendship, with the whole neighborhood.[28]

"House-raisings," as such occasions were called, were major social events on the Southern frontier. While the men built the house, the women prepared a big meal, and when the work was done there was always a party to make the newcomer feel at home. Newlyweds and those whose homes were struck by fire also benefited from the custom.

Cooperative labor was required for clearing land or burning off weeds prior to farming and was especially important at harvest time. The job of husking corn, for example, was too large for a family, and the whole neighborhood turned out to participate in a "corn-shucking," which usually took the form of a race. The corn was divided into two equal piles, and two teams with captains chosen by the host vied to finish first in getting their piles shucked. Inevitably the host would produce enough whiskey to go around as the competition progressed, and the more whiskey was consumed, the greater was the tempo of the work. When one of the teams emerged the winner, in the words of Kentucky pioneer Dr. Daniel Drake:

> the victorious captain, mounted on the shoulders of some of the stoutest men, with the bottle in one hand and his hat in the other, was carried in triumph around the vanquished party amidst shouts of victory which rent the air.
>
> Then came the supper on which the women had been busily employed and which always included a "pot pie." Either before or after eating the fighting took place & by midnight the sober were found assisting the drunken home.[29]

[28] Quoted by Buck in *Illinois in 1818*, 67.
[29] Daniel Drake, M.D., *Pioneer Life in Kentucky, 1785–1800*, ed. Emmet Field Horine, M.D., 56.

Another form of corn-shucking which was not competitive has been described by the Reverend George Brewer of Coosa County, Alabama. The participants gathered around a pile of unshucked corn, and as they worked they drank and sang the "corn-songs" which usually accompanied the task.

> There were usually two or more recognized leaders in singing the corn songs, and as they would chant or shout their couplet, all the rest would join in the chorus. There was no poetry or metre to these songs, but there was a thrill from the melody welling up with such earnestness from the singers that it was so inspiring that the hands would fly with rapidity in tearing off the shucks, and the feet would kick back the shucks with equal vigor. The leader would shout:
> "Pull off the shucks boys, pull off the shucks,"
> the crowd [would] shout out in a chorus:
> "Round up the corn, boys, round up the corn."
> The leader would then chant:
> "The night's getting off boys, the night's getting off"
> The crowd would again sing the chorus:
> "Round up the corn boys, round up the corn"
> ... This singing could be heard on a still night 2 miles.[30]

Even the pattern of the song contributed to cooperation by coordinating the participants' work.

The women, too, used social events to get their work done. Farm women had to work alongside their husbands in the fields when agricultural demands were pressing, and plain-folk society allowed women few roles beyond those of wife and mother.[31] There were

---

[30] Owsley, *Plain Folk*, 113. Interestingly, it is easier to find accounts of corn-shuckings among black Southerners than among whites. Several of the ex-slaves interviewed by the WPA in the 1930s had fond memories of corn-shuckings, and give brief accounts of both cooperative and competitive events; see Norman R. Yetman, ed., *Life under the "Peculiar Institution": Selections from the Slave Narrative Collection*, esp. 62, 190. A corn song similar to the one recorded here can be found in W. F. Allen, Charles P. Ware, and Lucy McKim Garrison, *Slave Songs of the United States*, 68. One can only guess at the direction of influence.

[31] Anne Firor Scott, *The Southern Lady*, 35.

some activities, however—exclusively "women's work"—which were organized cooperatively. Some of these tasks supplemented cooperative labor by the men, as when the women of the neighborhood prepared food for a house-raising or corn-shucking. On those occasions, nevertheless, the role of the women was clearly subordinated to that of their husbands, for they had to wait upon the table while the men dined and could themselves eat only when the men were finished.[32] Other, more exclusively female activities such as furnishing a new house or spinning yarn required the cooperation of several women for their accomplishment, and such events as the spinning bee were quite popular on the Southern frontier. Though those tasks could easily be taken on by one woman or two, the social atmosphere must have provided a welcome antidote to the discomfort and tedium of household work.

When people in a neighborhood decided to move on, they continued to depend on their neighbors because it was common for people to travel in groups. Many migrating bands were formed in the original neighborhood when families joined together or when organizations such as church congregations moved west intact. Others were formed by impresarios specifically for colonization of new lands; Texas, in particular, received many such groups. Sometimes several hundred in number, these migrating groups were necessary for the mutual support and common defense of all participants; individual travel through unknown regions would have been a difficult if not impossible undertaking.[33]

Closely related was the well-documented phenomenon of Southern hospitality, particularly among the plain-folk. Olmsted, having noted a lack of hospitality on the part of planters, except among their own kind, found quite the opposite reception in his dealings with frontier farmers who were willing to offer the best they had, demanding no pay.[34] In fact, frontier hospitality encompassed more than a free hot meal and a place to sleep. Custom on the frontier legalized many acts that would have been regarded

[32] Owsley, *Plain Folk*, 107.
[33] Boatright, "Frontier Individualism," 45–46.
[34] Olmsted, *Journey in the Back Country*, 32, 204.

as trespass in more densely populated areas. There was an unwritten law that no bona fide traveler who killed game along his route could be prosecuted for poaching. The traveler could enter a house in the absence of the owner, take what food he needed, and not worry about being punished by a frontier court. He might even take kitchen privileges so long as he cleaned up after himself.[35]

Cooperative work groups, group migration, and hospitality were not simply products of the plain-folk's innate altruism. Instead, each phenomenon stemmed from needs growing out of the insecurities of life on the frontier. Some of the work of farming was more demanding than one family could have handled. In times of emergency, as when a house burned down, the stricken farmer was almost entirely dependent on outside help, and the difficulties of travel on the frontier made companions and hospitable resting places indispensable. The individual, in turn, was obligated to hold himself in readiness to return these favors whenever a need arose for his services or for those of anyone in his family. Plain-folk participated in a community life not so much out of goodness or even because they expected to be repaid in kind, but for a sense of security that came from knowing they could count on others in time of need.

Yet the frontier's social security[36] rested on an unstable base. If cooperation was an important part of frontier life, so was competition. Even cooperative activities were often organized competitively, and the rivalries were keen. One frontiersman remembered that corn-shuckings had taught him that competition "is the mother of cheating, falsehood, and broils." Corn was surreptitiously moved into opponents' piles or thrown into the crib unshucked. Should a cheater be caught, he would counter by calling his accuser a liar, and a fight was sure to ensue.[37]

The competitive spirit also entered into recreation. Horseracing, gambling, cockfighting, and athletics were the major activities—

---

[35] Boatright, "Frontier Individualism," 49.
[36] Ibid., 48.
[37] Drake, *Pioneer Life*, 55–56.

all were taken quite seriously. A measure of the seriousness can be seen in the following incident that, according to Guion Johnson, occurred in ante-bellum North Carolina:

> In 1810 . . . a young man dropped dead while playing a game of fives [a type of handball] at a muster near Warrenton. He had previously fainted twice and his friends had urged him to stop playing; but, fearing the taunts to which an indication of physical weakness would subject him, he remained in the field, declaring that he would finish that game if he never played another.[38]

The incident may have been unusual, but it was only the logical extension of an important aspect of plain-folk life.

This competitiveness was part of the frontiersman's image of himself as an individualist. It was an image basic to the plain-folk's beliefs about themselves, expressed most succinctly in folklore through the heroes of their stories. Although no single epic hero emerged on the frontier, a hero type did develop in oral tradition and was later immortalized in almanacs and in the works of the Southwestern humorists. Typically, the hero was a man who was self-reliant, scornful of formal institutions, and tough enough to take on any foe.

The plain-folk chose their heroes from many areas of life. Some, like David Crockett, were real men, close to frontier experiences, while others were drawn from groups with which the farmers were likely to have contact, such as the flatboatman Mike Fink or the jackleg preacher immortalized by Western journalist William Penn Brannan.[39] An additional group of heroes, taken from outside the pale of respectable society, included outlaws, con men, and gamblers. Still another frontier folk hero, Andrew Jackson, reached the Presidency of the United States. For all their apparent diversity, however, these heroes embodied the common set of

---

[38] Guion Griffis Johnson, *Ante-Bellum North Carolina*, 109.

[39] Two of Brannan's "sermons" are printed in *Humor in the Old Southwest*, ed. Hennig Cohen and William B. Dillingham, 355–59. B. A. Botkin reports having collected one of these sermons from oral tradition in North Carolina, 1949, in *A Treasury of Southern Folklore*, 112n.

characteristics that came to be known as frontier individualism.

A primary aspect of frontier individualism was a belief in self-reliance, that each individual could control his own fate. Like Crockett or Fink, he might overcome insuperable odds with brute force and a modicum of cunning, or the hero might con a whole community with his gift for words—as when Brannan's preacher had "every Hard Shell Baptist shell out."[40] And the frontiersman particularly liked such men as Crockett and Jackson who rose from humble circumstances to positions of economic and political prominence. Not incidentally, both Crockett and Jackson were highly regarded for their opposition to the entrenched speculator interests in the South, although Jackson's reputation was more legend than fact—he himself was something of a speculator.[41]

Coupled with self-reliance was a disdain for formal institutions. To the plain-folk, the frontier stood for personal freedom and a life unfettered by the artificial restraints of "civilization"; hence, frontier heroes were men of action rather than the subjects of rules. The backwoods hero—the fabled "hunter of Kentucky"— who accompanied Andy Jackson at the battle of New Orleans had not needed military discipline to rout the British troops but could rely on native strength and ability for success. He and his descendants would never have much use for the conventions of society when it came to righting wrongs and deflating civilized pretensions. Indeed, it is not surprising that frontier folk would honor bandits, scalawags, ne'er-do-wells, and gamblers, as well as those who, like Crockett and Jackson, succeeded on society's terms. Nor is it surprising that vigilantism, rather than duly constituted courts, provided the frontier answer to law and order, with "justice" dispensed quickly and with violence.[42]

[40] Cohen and Dillingham, *Humor*, 359.

[41] John William Ward, *Andrew Jackson—Symbol for an Age*, 41–45, 167. Constance Rourke, *American Humor*, 53. Marvin Meyers, *The Jacksonian Persuasion*, 22.

[42] Richard Maxwell Brown, "The American Vigilante Tradition," in *Violence in America*, ed. Hugh Davis Graham and Ted Robert Gurr, 154–226 passim. See also in the same volume, Joe B. Frantz, "The Frontier Tradition: An Invitation to Violence," 128–31. Specifically, Southern "justice" is described by Everett Dick in *The Dixie Frontier*, 226.

In fact, the plain-folk had only slight control over their ability to achieve success and security, given the Southern environment. Further, the need to cooperate in neighborhood activities constrained the frontier farmer's ability to act spontaneously and without restraint. As a result, plain-folk individualism took a turn of the kind W. J. Cash ascribed to the whole of Southern society when he wrote:

> . . . the individualism of the plantation world would be one which, like that of the backcountry before it, would be far too much concerned with bold, immediate, unsupported aggression of the ego, which placed too great stress on the inviolability of personal whim, and which was full of the chip-on-the-shoulder swagger and brag of a boy—one, in brief, of which the essence was the boast, voiced or not, on the part of every Southerner, that he would knock hell out of whoever dared to cross him.[43]

Cut off from his primary goals of self-sufficiency and success, the frontier individualist turned to other outlets. Some were competitive sports like horseracing and cockfighting, but the one of greatest importance was fighting. Plain-folk heroes were almost always bullies and fighters, and the frontiersman was himself ready to attack at the drop of a hat. A letter written in Virginia in 1809 gives a fairly typical account:

> . . . a few evenings ago a disagreeable occurrence happened between Wm. Garrett and Mathew Wells they split a difference about buying wine—which soon grew to a very passionate quarrel; when Garret drew out his knife and swore if he was rushed upon he would stab him. Wells then came near him not seeing the knife (a dim fire light) rushed in upon him; which terminated in five or six stabs recd. by Wells—but fortunately not fatal—two in his Belly (not deep) one or two in his thigh (very deep and bled much) behind his shoulder—in his head &c.[44]

Whenever members of the community gathered, be it on court day or at a crossroads store, the would-be champion was wont to

43 Cash, *Mind of the South*, 42–43.
44 In Phillips, *Plantation and Frontier*, II, 295.

strut about, boasting of his fighting prowess. The bait was invariably taken, resulting in either a rugged wrestling match or, more often, a gouging match. Each combatant used punching, kicking, and biting to defeat and physically maim his opponent, but the acme of accomplishment came in the gouging. According to the Irish traveler Isaac Weld, "To perform the horrid operation, the combatant twists his forefingers in the side locks of his adversary's hair, and then applies his thumbs to the bottom of the eye, to force it out of the socket."[45] If this could not be done, then a severe scratching would have to suffice. Fighting was a serious problem in the Old South: in one North Carolina county in 1839, for example, all but three of sixty-nine indictments were for assault and battery.[46]

A variety of explanations has been advanced to account for the role of violence in both frontier tradition and behavior. That it was in large measure because of the use of liquor as a panacea for the hard conditions of life is beyond doubt, but it is not enough to attribute ante-bellum Southern drinking and fighting to some kind of regression to savagery. In fact, both the violent hero type and the aggressive, hedonistic behaviors occur in many groups which are kept out of the social and economic mainstream and for which daily, ongoing cooperation is important. Posing the threat of defiant noncooperation, the acts of the brutal antisocial hero represent the last stand of such a people against an oppressive system. In addition, while toughness was a virtue in those who had to endure the frontier environment, its assertion was also an attempt to find one area, at least, in which manly self-reliance could be realized.

The need for cooperation, urgent as it was, could not submerge the frontier emphasis on individual self-reliance and spontaneity of action. As long as cooperation was not congruent with the plain-folk's self-image, then the need to participate in neighborhood work and the dependence upon one's neighbors were likely to have been sources of tension in frontier communities. Violent

---

[45] *Travels Through the States of North America*, 2 vols., I, 192.
[46] Johnson, *Ante-Bellum North Carolina*, 42.

acts were not directed toward any particular goal, other than maiming one's opponent, so that the fight was an end in itself. Nor was ante-bellum fighting based on any group ties, as later feuds would be, but simply took place among individuals whenever the neighborhood came together. Thus, fighting on the frontier may best be undertsood as a way in which the tensions inherent in plain-folk life were released, as each participant asserted not only his abilities, but also his autonomy.[47]

Added to the contradiction between the value placed on individualism and the need to cooperate with one's neighbors was of course the contradiction to be found in the discrepancy between expectations and the possibility of their satisfaction. Each type of contradiction contributed to a way of life that was remarkably tense and unstable, one in which goals and hopes were seldom realized and one in which the individual's proper relationships with his neighbors were not clear and were thus highly unpredictable. Most of the plain-folk simply accepted the situation; many found release in drinking and violent "sports." But for some a better solution was found in frontier religious sects.

Religion on the Southern frontier, particularly Methodist and Baptist religion, developed within a context of tension and instability and offered the plain-folk an alternative way of life. Institutionally, the sects provided a disciplined community in which proper relationships between individuals were spelled out and rules rigidly enforced, just as the internal affairs of the sects provided an alternative sphere of action where people could assert themselves in ways other than those denied them by secular Southern society. The sect provided a different society in which the contradictions of frontier life no longer occurred.

But this was only one dimension of frontier religion, for it was, after all, primarily religious rather than social. It is doubtful that anyone became a Methodist or a Baptist because he wanted an

[47] Interesting and useful comparative data on hero types can be found in E. J. Hobsbawm, *Primitive Rebels*, esp. 24–25. For a comparative perspective on violent behavior which emphasizes questions of group ties and of goals, see Charles Tilly, "Collective Violence in European Perspective," in *Violence in America*, ed. Graham and Gurr, 4–45.

arena in which to gain status or to have his social life regulated. Most people joined for religious reasons, especially out of a desire for salvation and a life to come, and the religious belief system also contributed to the resolution of tensions and instabilities in plain-folk life. Frontier religious beliefs provided, on the one hand, a set of alternative goals, since those of the dominant society were essentially unattainable to most frontier farmers. More importantly, the religious beliefs constituted a new view of the world, offering the believer a different way of looking at himself and those around him.

II

RELIGION IS A FORTUNE

Religion in Frontier Society

A T THE OPENING of the nineteenth century, the Methodist and Baptist churches occupied a small place in Southern frontier religious life. Most of those who lived on the frontier were unchurched, and if any religious organization could be said to be dominant, it was the Presbyterian church, for much of the backcountry was settled by Scotch-Irish and Scottish Presbyterians. Nevertheless, as Southerners moved into Kentucky and the Old Southwest, the Presbyterians found their efforts duplicated and even exceeded by those of the Methodists and Baptists. Ministers of both the latter sects had, in fact, preceded Presbyterian clergymen into Kentucky and the Southwest, and both organizations were steadily to overtake Presbyterianism in ministering to plain-folk.

The relative progress of each group on the frontier resulted from individual patterns of organization and from the goals held by their representatives. The Presbyterians were by far the most conservative in their practices with regard to the ministry and in their theology. Only the Presbyterians, of the three groups, had any concern for an educated clergy, at least in the early days on the frontier. A college degree or its equivalent was required for ordination as a Presbyterian minister, and many of the earliest ministers in Kentucky and Tennessee were Princeton graduates. In some ways this requirement was beneficial to the people of the frontier, since it served as an impetus for the founding of formal educational institutions in new areas—the Transylvania Seminary, for example, was set up by Kentucky Presbyterians in 1783[1]—but the desire for an educated ministry was to have an important effect on the ability of the Presbyterians to operate effectively in frontier society. The sermons of their educated ministers were often deeply intellectual in content, having been carefully prepared well in advance of delivery, and the ministers focused on scriptural exposition and creedal niceties. While this kind of preaching may have suited the tastes of the prosperous, literate members of many of the congregations, the importance of theological complexities was often lost on the poorer folk.

Further, the means by which the Presbyterian ministry moved west differed significantly from Baptist and Methodist practices in that the majority of Presbyterian ministers went strictly on invitation from previously established congregations. The first Presbyterian minister did not enter Kentucky until he had received a call from three already established congregations to provide for his support, and the same was true of most others: in 1794, for example, Joseph P. Howe was called by the churches at Little Mountain and Springfield, Kentucky; with the two congregations he would receive £100 sterling, one-third in cash and two-thirds in "Marchantable produce."[2] The "calling procedure," as it was known, limited the growth and progress of Presbyterianism on the frontier, for the fact that one had to be invited to minister to a frontier congregation meant that Presbyterian ministers went to the frontier to serve Presbyterians and had little or no concern with attracting new members from the ranks of those who were affiliated with other churches or had no church affiliation at all. The limits this practice placed on the potential of the denomination for growth are indicated by the fact that by 1820, when Kentucky Baptists and Methodists could *each* claim about 21,000 members, Presbyterians numbered only 2,700.[3]

The Baptists not only did not require that their ministers be

---

[1] William Warren Sweet, *Religion on the American Frontier*, II, *The Presbyterians*, 74.

[2] Walter Brownlow Posey, *The Presbyterian Church in the Old Southwest, 1778–1838*, 39.

[3] Sweet, *Presbyterians*, 33.

educated, but valued a lack of education as a positive ministerial attribute. Conversion, a direct experience of salvation believed to be initiated by the Lord, was the crucial qualification for the ministry, as it was for church membership. Such a direct experience of God's power was felt to be far superior to any enlightenment that might be gained from a worldly education. Unlike Presbyterian clergymen, who performed their duties as a profession, many Baptist ministers were farmer-preachers who earned their livelihoods by farming, serving their congregations on the side. Their sermons were "almost altogether hortatory," deriving eloquence not so much from preparation as from the direct inspiration of the Holy Spirit.[4]

As farmer-preachers, Baptist ministers did not wait for a call but moved west with their congregations. Such a Baptist migration to the West as that of the Gilbert's Creek Church of Kentucky was not unusual. The church went to Kentucky in a body, led by their minister. They maintained their organization, with the minister preaching as they camped along the way and performing several baptisms in the mountain streams. When they reached their new home in December 1781, they gathered for worship "around the same old Bible they had used back in Spottsylvania," in Virginia.[5] Additionally, ordination procedures were carried out by individual congregations, the only real criterion being eloquence as demonstrated by an effective "exercise" of one's "gifts" before the congregation, although, of course, there was some concern for good behavior and doctrinal orthodoxy.

More to the point, Baptists, unlike Presbyterians, preached to everyone. Effective service to his own congregation accounted for only part of the Baptist preacher's duties, for he was also expected to bring unchurched neighbors into the fold through a variety of missionary activities. Although this outreach was not approved by all Baptists, leading to minor schisms in some places, Baptist missionaries met with great success, and the church grew from a minor body at the beginning of the nineteenth century to a position as the second Southern church by the time of the Civil War, serving from one-quarter to one-third of Southern church members.[6]

The Methodists, largely as a result of effective organization, were to become the major Southern church in 1860. Like the Baptists, they relied on an uneducated but converted ministry throughout their early history, but they also had a hierarchical administrative structure, and Methodist preachers, like their Presbyterian counterparts, performed their duties full time, albeit for smaller material rewards. Moreover, unlike either of the other two groups, the Methodist central organization *sent* ministers into the new territories for the express purpose of gathering in new members.

The Methodist hierarchy consisted of bishops, elders, and preachers, each with a particular area of jurisdiction, and each preacher was beholden to the hierarchy rather than to a local congregation. In its provision for some degree of central control, the organization was more effective than that of the Baptists, but it also provided for a looser relationship between the minister and his congregation. On the frontier the Methodist preachers were itinerants who covered large areas and served numerous local groups. A single circuit might involve the itinerant, or "circuit rider," on a journey as great as five hundred miles, and it could take a traveling preacher six weeks or more to reach all those who desired his ministry. The Methodist itineracy was an arduous and dangerous occupation, but by spreading its message over large territories at a time when settlement was sparse, Methodism developed rapidly. It is a measure of the sect's success that while in the years immediately following the Revolution the Methodists were much maligned and even persecuted for their identification with the Loyalist cause—probably because of the strong Toryism of John Wesley—by 1830 Methodism had reached parity with the other denominations in the South, and by 1860 it accounted for

---

[6] Statistics in Walter Brownlow Posey, *Frontier Mission*, 417–21.

MAP 2. The Kentucky circuit traveled by Jacob Young as an itinerant on the Salt River Circuit, 1802.

from 40 to 50 percent of the overall church membership, state by state.[7] Differences in theology also had much to do with the relative progress of each group. The Presbyterians, by and large, stuck to their own tough and closely reasoned brand of Calvinism; the Baptists too, were Calvinistic, though they showed less interest in close reasoning. The Methodists preached a doctrine of free grace and free salvation, and their Arminianism alone has often been cited as a cause of Methodist successes on the frontier. It may have been true that the Methodist preachers had but slight concern for the difficulties posed by Wesley's complex ideas of free grace, but all could expound for hours on man's mastery of his own fate— and on Calvinist religion's lack of common sense. Such appeals to common sense and the insistence upon man's freedom accorded well with frontier values, no doubt contributing much to the ultimate primacy of Methodism in the Old South. So great, in fact, was the success of Methodism, and so attractive were its teachings to plain-folk, that only the strictest frontier Calvinists among the Baptists and Presbyterians were able to resist a shift toward the Arminian position. Even in the early days of frontier evangelism, Presbyterian preachers stressed the role of human choice in individual salvation, so that the preaching of Methodist itinerants came to take over Southern religion to a degree that church rolls can only partially make plain.[8]

To whom, in fact, did the various religious groups appeal? The Presbyterians had something of a head start in evangelism because many of the early frontier settlers were already members of that organization; frontier Presbyterianism, however, was plagued by class divisions from the beginning. A serious split, debated on theological terms, which reflected those class divisions, led to the formation of the Cumberland Presbyterian church as an independent organization in 1810. Although conservative Presby-

[7] Statistics for 1830 in Andrew Reed and James Matheson, *A Narrative of the Visit to the American Churches, by the Deputation from the Congregational Union of England and Wales*, 2 vols., II, 363. Statistics for 1860 in Posey, *Frontier Mission*, 417–21.
[8] John B. Boles, *The Great Revival, 1787–1805*, 138.

terians saw the split as resulting from the adoption of "Methodist Arminianism" by a small number of individual ministers,[9] in fact the causes were much deeper. Practices of ordination as well as theology were at stake, for since 1802 the Cumberland Presbytery had engaged in licensing uneducated but converted clergymen. In part, the practice grew out of frontier needs since it was not easy to attract educated men to the frontier—particularly to less prosperous congregations—but the dispute also reflected the hostility between small farmer Presbyterians and the eastern-oriented church leadership. The more orthodox leadership of the Presbyterian church was quite unprepared to sacrifice traditional practices to frontier needs, nor were Presbyterian leaders particularly interested in expanding the church's outreach through the ordination of uneducated men to spread the gospel. In thus reacting to Cumberland practices through the censure of those involved, the old-line leaders essentially separated themselves from any direct concern for the religious welfare of frontier folk.[10]

Presbyterianism in 1800 might better be classified as a religion on the frontier than as a frontier religion. To be sure, many plain-folk were Presbyterians, but by inheritance more than choice. The denomination itself was more in tune with the lives of planters—indeed, many of the called clergy were planter-speculators on the side[11]—and its leaders were educated professionals who identified their interests with those of the Southern elite. Therefore, many of the orthodoxies of Presbyterianism simply put the body out of touch with the plain-folk, leading on occasion to major schisms, but more often to a great number of individual defections to more representative groups.

With the Methodists and Baptists such divisions, though not unknown, were never so important. The Baptist church was definitely a frontier organization that ministered to the plain-folk. Preachers were drawn from the ranks of the congregation, and

[9] See, for example, Robert Davidson, *History of the Presbyterian Church in the State of Kentucky*, 166.

[10] H. Richard Niebuhr, *The Social Sources of Denominationalism*, 158–59. See also Boles, *Great Revival*, 160–61.

[11] Posey, *Presbyterian Church*, 39.

congregations themselves were comprised initially of small farmers who had migrated from older areas. Further, the Baptists drew much strength from gathering in the unchurched and dissatisfied members from other churches, particularly Presbyterians. So close were the Baptists to the feelings and thoughts of plain-folk that many frontier Presbyterians did choose to become Baptists, either en masse as in the case of the Campbellite schism of 1813, when a large group of Kentucky Presbyterians chose to enter the Baptist fold,[12] or as individuals seeking religious satisfaction.

Still, the preeminent frontier religious organization was the Methodist Episcopal church. Although Methodists had drawn some support from the upper class before the Revolution, when the group was a movement within Anglicanism, by the turn of the century the Wesleyan faith had come to be scorned by the "cultured" as a religion for blacks and poor whites, and planters began to return to the Protestant Episcopal church. In some parts of the South during the early years of the nineteenth century, elite Episcopalians even attempted to prevent Methodists from setting up churches.[13] Many of the theological and practical issues which drove frontier folk out of the Presbyterian church in the early part of the century had already been resolved by Methodism in their favor: the church was committed to Arminian theology and made good use of an uneducated (though sometimes self-educated), converted clergy. So the Methodists, like the Baptists, drew much of their strength from dissatisfied Presbyterians. The story told by the itinerant Jacob Young is not unusual and illustrates both frontier life and Methodist success. Young was born in Allegheny County, Pennsylvania, in 1776. His father was Anglican; his mother, Presbyterian, and Jacob was raised in the latter faith. At the age of fifteen he was taken by his parents to the Kentucky frontier, and a few years later he first came into contact with Methodist preaching, causing him to question his Presbyterian beliefs:

[12] Niebuhr, *Social Sources*, 169.
[13] G. G. Johnson, *Ante-Bellum North Carolina*, 348, 430; Rosser Howard Taylor, *Ante-Bellum South Carolina*, 153.

> I had read the old Westminster Confession of Faith, in the light of the Bible, with a view to know if the doctrine of Calvinism was a doctrine of Scripture. I thought if I could but satisfy myself that Calvinism is true, I would be at ease; but this I could not do. It was as clearly as that two and two make four, that if the Bible was true, the old Confession was false.[14]

It was but a short time thereafter that Young joined the Methodist fold, later to become one of the church's most able itinerants.

Young's background could not have been closer to the pattern of frontier life, and something similar was recounted by just about all of the itinerants who left autobiographies (leading one to suspect that even if their accounts were not completely true, there was a kind of plain-folk norm to Methodism). Most itinerants were the sons of small farmers who moved early from the Eastern states of Pennsylvania, Virginia, and North Carolina into Kentucky and Tennessee, though after the consolidation of the plantation system in those states, many left the South for Illinois, Ohio, or Indiana. Their leadership could only have strengthened the ties of Methodism to the people of the frontier.

At the opening of the nineteenth century, then, three religious organizations competed for the souls of frontier folk. The Presbyterians began the century in a commanding position, but were already racked by dissensions growing out of class divisions within the organization. Never wholly belonging to the frontier farmers and identified closely with the planters, Presbyterianism virtually dropped out of the competition early on, and by 1860, only about 7 percent of Southern church members were Presbyterians.[15]

Both the Methodist and Baptist churches drew to their ranks not only the previously unchurched, but also disgruntled members from the more conservative Presbyterian denomination. In the beginning they identified closely with the farmers, and those preachers who left autobiographies show a clear pattern of frontier origins and a way of secular life typical of the frontier. The continuing emphasis on evangelism meant that both organizations

---

14 Jacob Young, *Autobiography of a Pioneer*, 23–39. Quotation on 39.
15 Posey, *Frontier Mission*, 417–21.

would remain in contact with the frontier and its way of life for many years, and it meant, too, that many of the functionaries in both organizations would be drawn from frontier people. Thus, for many years the Methodist and Baptist churches belonged distinctly to the people of the Southern frontier.

Yet, if the two organizations belonged primarily to the plain-folk, not all plain-folk belonged to them, nor to any religious organization for that matter. The available statistics do not permit much precision in this area but do show that church members, of whatever class, were always in a minority in the ante-bellum South. In 1830 only about 10 percent of the people living in the old frontier states of Kentucky, Tennessee, Alabama, and Mississippi were members of the major Protestant denominations, a figure consistent with other Southern states and, in fact, with the rest of the nation. By 1860 the proportion had risen to about 20 percent—an increase—but church members still comprised a minority of Southerners.[16] In fact, Southerners generally displayed a good deal of apathy and even hostility toward organized religion. A traveler to the region in 1808 wrote:

> The gentlemen pass their time in the pursuit of three things: all make love; most of them play; and a few make money. With Religion they have nothing to do; having formed a treaty with her, the principle article of which is, "Trouble us not, nor will we trouble you."[17]

When Matthew P. Sturdivant went as the first Methodist missionary to the Tombigbee country (Alabama) in 1808, the result of his first year's labor was that not a single member was enrolled into the Methodist church, although in his second year he was able to convert eighty-six.[18]

Even worse than apathy was the open hostility faced by the bearers of the word. Although the itinerants were dependent upon

---

[16] Ibid.; Reed and Matheson, *Visit to the American Churches* II, 363.

[17] In Francis A. Cabaniss and James A. Cabaniss, "Religion in Ante-Bellum Mississippi," *Journal of Mississippi History* 6 (1944), 200.

[18] Marion Elias Lazenby, *History of Methodism in Alabama and West Florida*, 37, 46.

the goodness of the people for their survival, Southern hospitality did not always extend to preachers. Quite to the contrary, they were often charged exorbitant rates for their lodgings, were mocked, and were even denied the privilege of praying, being threatened with bodily harm if they did not leave. On occasion they were run out of town, as in the case of a Baptist minister who was rowed across the river from St. Stephens, Alabama, and threatened with a tarring-and-feathering if he ever returned. Although St. Stephens was in an area populated by many Catholics, the hostility did not stem from any sectarian bias: the Catholic church had been converted to a brothel.[19]

Hostility was even more vividly shown in an apparent frontier tradition in which drunken ruffians attempted to disrupt religious gatherings. With the support of hard liquor, which was cheap and plentiful, many a man became bold enough to challenge those who would be saved, and some states even had to pass laws to prevent disorderly conduct at places of worship by forbidding drunkenness, swearing, and the vending of liquor anywhere near a religious gathering. As if that were not enough, the churches had to contend with lawlessness perpetrated by local bandits who learned that one way to disarm an intended victim was to assume the dress of an itinerant. The bandit John A. Murrel, who was something of a folk hero, reported on the usefulness of scriptural knowledge acquired in prison and on the value of preaching ability for his "speculation." He recounted that on one trip through Georgia he robbed only eleven men, but, he said, "I preached some d——d fine sermons, and scattered some counterfeit United States' paper among my brethren."[20]

Because the churches were obviously not for everyone, they must have drawn their memberships from a particular segment of plain-folk society. These were people for whom frontier hedonism could not have been attractive and who sought stability and re-

---

[19] Albert Burton Moore, *History of Alabama and Her People*, 181–82.

[20] From portions of Murrel's memoirs reprinted in Botkin, ed., *Treasury of Southern Folklore* 222, 224. A variant is quoted in Cabaniss and Cabaniss, "Religion," 201.

spectability in their lives.[21] Such people found means for counter-
ing the hedonism of their society through participation in frontier
religious organizations. Neither the Methodist nor the Baptist
church neglected the social side of its ministry, and both organizations attained a remarkable degree of success in their continuing
campaigns against "immorality."

According to Methodist itinerant Peter Cartwright, there was
"a trinity of devils to fight, namely, superfluous dress, whisky, and
slavery,"[22] but the list could be extended to include such popular
diversions as horseracing, the theater, gambling, and dancing. To
some extent this catalogue of sins may be characterized as a
protest morality of the disinherited, based on the class consciousness of frontier religion.[23] Their moral protestations were directed
at several activities in which the planter elite engaged. Conspicu-
ous consumption was the hallmark of planter life, and the strong
opposition to slavery present in both denominations during the
early nineteenth century may well have reflected the resentment
of nonslaveholding farmers toward the planters as a class.

Still, such activities as drinking, gambling, swearing, and horseracing were also favorite pastimes on the frontier and were the
very activities especially inimical to social cohesion and stability.
Horseracing and gambling were conducive to competition; fancy
dress, to economic differentiation within the group; and drinking,
perhaps the most serious sin, contributed significantly to frontier
violence. By directing their attention toward such activities, the
church-folk were focusing directly on sources of community instability and frontier tensions.

The bans on immoral activities were made known in several
ways, including education. The early preachers, particularly the
Presbyterians and even the Methodists, comprised the only edu-

---

[21] A similar group was identified in the black community of Chicago by
St. Clair Drake and Horace R. Cayton, *Black Metropolis*, 2 vols., II, 524–25.
There is a clear analogy between those "church-centered respectables," as Drake
and Cayton termed them, and the kind of people who were likely to have been
drawn to the frontier sects.

[22] Peter Cartwright, *Autobiography of Peter Cartwright, the Backwoods
Preacher*, 95.

[23] Don Yoder, *Pennsylvania Spirituals*, 102.

cative influence brought to bear on frontier society, and as they taught reading and writing, they served up heavy doses of moral teachings. They also dwelt on moral themes in their sermons. The best sermon, in frontier days as always, was one which hit close to the heart by focusing on a topic that was relevant to the everyday life of the individual in order to expose his sins and, hence, bring him to repentance.

But the frontier churches were not content to rely on education to control their members. Instead, Methodists and Baptists, as well as Presbyterians, developed and enforced church disciplines. To some extent the disciplines displayed creedal and doctrinal concerns and gave rules for trials on charges concerning heresy. The frontier churches were, however, equally concerned with regulating their members' social behavior, and charges of misconduct in economic or social affairs figured prominently in church trials. The churches have rightly been called "frontier moral courts."[24] Even with all their expulsions on theological grounds, for example, the Baptists of the Southern frontier could attribute about half their actions to charges of drunkenness.[25]

Each of the sects, Methodist and Baptist, had its own way of handling problems. The Baptists' disciplinary proceedings reflected their acknowledged democratic proclivities, and there were a series of "gospel steps" which had to be taken prior to the disciplining of any member. First, offender and offended attempted to settle their differences in a face-to-face confrontation; second, the parties called on the assistance of several witnesses; and finally, if these two steps produced no settlement, the matter was brought before the whole congregation. Although the pastor served as moderator, the entire membership was allowed to participate in the proceedings, and the accused could be expelled only on the unanimous vote of all present; in some associations, however, a two-thirds majority was considered sufficient. The chief public offenses were drunkenness, cursing, and fighting, with private complaints in-

[24] William Warren Sweet, *Religion in the Development of American Culture, 1765–1840,* 137.

[25] Posey, *Frontier Mission,* 304.

cluding wife-beating and child neglect. Civil issues within the churches' jurisdiction included repudiation of contracts, abuse of another's livestock, and fraud.[26]

The Methodist system was more structured. Each local society was divided into classes grouped according to neighborhood, and each class had the duty to observe whether its members were faithfully persevering toward salvation. This perseverance involved, among other things, following the formal Discipline of the Methodist Episcopal Church. The Discipline was rigorous and comprehensive, covering church practices, doctrine, and individual behavior. Not only did it deal with the usual issues of intemperance and fighting, but it even provided for a probationary period for Methodists who married outside the denomination. In the instance of a possible lawsuit between two church members, the action had to be submitted to a deacon before being taken to a secular court. Failure to do so could result in the suspension of either or both parties. There were also injunctions against haggling, usurious interest, and fraud, all of which could seriously threaten the cohesion of the community. Committees to try any charges were held before the bishop, and even nonmembers could testify. Those found guilty of serious offenses could be expelled, and minor offenders received at least a reprimand.[27]

Both the Baptist and Methodist organizations were aided in their efforts to maintain order by their sectarian, noninclusive composition. Both required that anyone who would be a church member give definite evidence of having experienced conversion, thus limiting their memberships only to those who had been saved by what was believed to be the direct intervention of the Lord, and also only to those who had evidenced a genuine desire to become a part of the group. It was not enough that one recite a catechism, for anyone could learn to repeat a set of propositions; a future member was also required to bear witness to having been saved. Even the Presbyterians were influenced by the sectarian tendencies

---

[26] T. Scott Miyakawa, *Protestants and Pioneers*, 22–23.

[27] Ibid., 53–57; Methodist Episcopal Church, *The Doctrines and Disciplines of the Methodist Episcopal Church.*

of frontier religion. One conservative denominational historian found the rise of "experimental religion" to be one of the more noxious aberrations brought on by the unsettled condition of the people in the early days of Kentucky Presbyterianism,[28] and the secessionist Cumberland church maintained "experimental" practices and sectarian organization even after it left the parent denomination.

The disciplines represented an attempt on the part of the religious groups to create an alternative to frontier society and to Southern society in general. The groups' effort to bypass such secular authorities as were present, as in the Methodist requirement that litigation be submitted to a deacon before being taken to court, indicates that the desire for an alternative was, in fact, conscious. The moral concern enforced by the sects provided that measure of stability which was lacking in day-to-day life on the frontier, and thus provided an answer to the tensions which plagued the farmers in their dealings with their neighbors. At the same time, the voluntarism at the basis of sectarianism was an important source of strength for the sects. It explains whatever coercive powers the sects had, because the threat of suspension or expulsion was a very real restraint to wrongdoing. The frontier groups were not known to be hesitant about using that power when it was required. Thus, institutionally the Methodist and Baptist churches, and to some extent even the Presbyterian church, provided an arena in which the rules for behavior were both quite explicit and rigidly enforced; by being so they answered many of the problems of frontier life.

Unfortunately, membership in the frontier sects never amounted to more than about one-fifth of the ante-bellum Southern population. That one-fifth found stability through the disciplines enforced by their churches and also found comfort in the knowledge that because they had experienced conversion they could look forward to an even better world to come. But the sects were not content to sit back and savor what they had received, for the evangelistic impulse was strong among both Methodists and Bap-

---

[28] Davidson, *History of the Presbyterian Church*, 132.

tists, and the organizations measured their success by counting converts. In part, those who had found stability in the disciplines might well have wanted to see their less disciplined neighbors brought under control. Evangelism, however, has always been part of Christianity: their neighbors' souls as much as their neighbors' behavior motivated the frontier sectarians' outreach. The problem was that other plain-folk had to be converted before they could share in the benefits of church membership, and the conversion of the whole society was a pretty tall order. It was to that task that many of the frontier religious leaders set themselves.

The Methodists were the most interested in, and the most successful at, gaining converts. Much of the success of the Methodists was due to their theology and organization, but it was also due in large measure to their exploitation of the frontier's unique contribution to Christian practice, the camp-meeting. Camp-meetings were annual gatherings at which people camped out for several days of preaching, praying, singing, and, above all, converting souls to "the way." Crowds often numbered in the thousands and came to the campsite from as far as fifty miles away. The camp-meeting was, by all accounts, a significant frontier practice.

Camp-meetings were first held around 1800 as a twofold response to frontier conditions. The most obvious stimulus was an environment in which people were sparsely settled and had neither the funds nor the wherewithal to erect church buildings. The camp-meeting, where church-folk gathered in a central location and made their own lodgings in tents, was clearly suited to such a situation. In addition, the opening years of the nineteenth century witnessed a Great Revival which grew up mainly on the Southern frontier, coinciding with a time of heavy migration into the new regions. The revival was a time of substantial growth on the part of the churches, and the camp-meeting was closely connected with that growth.

Surprisingly, the camp-meeting practice appears to have originated with the Presbyterians. The camp-meeting itself simply "grew up" with the frontier, so that one cannot be sure when the first one was held—outdoor preaching is as old as Christianity itself. It is likely that the first camp-meeting, lasting several days, was conducted by the Presbyterian minister James McGready in Kentucky in July 1800 at a revival of the Gasper River congregation.[29] An even greater gathering, and the one which did most to demonstrate the utility of the practice as a revival method, was held at Cane Ridge, Kentucky, in August 1801. This too was a Presbyterian affair, led by the later dissident Barton W. Stone, but Methodist preachers were among the leaders; indeed, many of the early camp-meetings were interdenominational. Estimates of attendance ranged from ten to twenty-five thousand, with people coming from Kentucky, Tennessee, and even the territory north of the Ohio River. Services lasted for six days, without intermission. To most onlookers, the scene was one of utter chaos. According to Peter Cartwright:

> the mighty power of God was displayed in a very extraordinary manner; many were moved to tears, and bitter and loud crying for mercy. . . . Hundreds fell prostrate under the mighty power of God, as men slain in battle. Stands were erected in the woods from which preachers of different Churches proclaimed repentance toward God and faith in our Lord Jesus Christ, and it was supposed, by eye and ear witnesses, that between one and two thousand souls were happily and powerfully converted to God during the meeting. . . . Here our camp-meetings took their rise.[30]

As it turned out, many of the early Presbyterian leaders who originated the camp-meeting later either were expelled from the church or left voluntarily; included among those was the Reverend Barton W. Stone.

The Methodists enthusiastically adopted the practice of camp-meetings. By 1802 Francis Asbury, the first American bishop, was mentioning them frequently in his journal, and the practice seemed to be moving toward full institutional status within the church, a status, however, which it was never to receive.[31] Asbury reported some four hundred camp-meetings during 1811 alone,[32]

---

29 Charles A. Johnson, *The Frontier Camp Meeting*, 37.
30 Cartwright, *Autobiography*, 30–31.
31 Emory Stevens Bucke, ed., *The History of American Methodism*, 516.
32 Sweet, *Story of Religion*, 229.

and the pattern of those later meetings followed the precedent set at Cane Ridge in having large attendance, in duration, and in drawing crowds from a large territory, although none ever equaled the original. Further, though they would become more orderly, later meetings were never to discard the kind of enthusiasm described by Cartwright.

There is a legendary picture of the camp-meeting as an extended emotional orgy, a picture not without foundation in fact. The conversions which took place at camp-meetings were highly visible, invariably accompanied by exhibitions of "acrobatic Christianity," including jerks, falling, dancing, and barking.[33] Indeed, such displays were taken as signs of conversion. Jerks had the greatest popularity. They developed slowly in the body; the forearm might begin to twitch spasmodically, and this would spread until every muscle was affected.[34] Not only was this sometimes dangerous to the person so affected, but also was quite contagious, the mere suggestion often serving to send a whole congregation into fits. Cartwright reports having seen five hundred people jerking in a single congregation at one time, and, according to him, there was only one possible remedy: "It was, on all occasions, my practice to recommend fervent prayer as a remedy, and it was almost universally proved an effectual antidote."[35] Not, of course, that all preachers were concerned with prevention; as one wrote:

It seems to me, from the best judgment I can form, that God hath seen proper to take this method to convince people that he will work in a way to show his power; and sent the jerks as a sign of the times, partly in judgement for the people's unbelief, and yet as a mercy to convict people of the divine realities.[36]

Compared to the falling exercise, however, the jerks seem relatively mild. The one who fell lay helpless for from fifteen minutes to twenty-four hours, sometimes perfectly motionless, sometimes convulsed, writhing and screaming. Others, having fallen, would

---

[33] C. A. Johnson, *Frontier Camp Meeting*, 56.
[34] Cleveland, *Great Revival*, 98.
[35] Cartwright, *Autobiography*, 51.
[36] Lorenzo Dow, *History of Cosmopolite*, 183.

lament their fate as sinners, or proclaim their hope and urge their friends to join them in salvation. This, too, was an extremely popular exercise, and the success of a meeting could be measured by the number of people who "fell before the power of God."

Emotionalism in the means of conversion led to much of the criticism directed at camp-meeting religion and caused the more staid denominations, including the Presbyterian, to shy away from the practice as immoral and irreligious. There was value, nevertheless, in such displays: the exercises provided a form of release from the frustrations of the farmers' workaday world as well as clear evidence of conversion. Because both the major camp-meeting sects required conversion as a basis for membership, such highly visible evidence was useful to them, and to the convert, in determining the fitness of an individual for the church.

The camp-meeting was also a major social event of frontier life, inasmuch as it offered an unparalleled occasion for all the people in a territory to gather for several days of social activity, unencumbered by a need to work. Indeed, the gathering took on the form of a "holy fair" or "religious holiday"[37] because the whole community turned out, religious and irreligious. But as with any fair, holy or otherwise, all of the activities of the campground were not of the variety desired by church leaders. An Alabama girl attending a camp-meeting wrote in a letter to a friend that she had acquired "many boy friends," and informed her friend that the girls had enjoyed themselves "more than ever before."[38] There seems little doubt, in fact, that the campground served a necessary function as the frontier courting-ground. Accordingly, for all the plain-dress edicts of the churches, it was not uncommon for the camp-meeting also to provide the setting for a ladies' dress parade. That the campground could be devoted to such a purpose so struck one old itinerant that he offered a parody upon the latest women's fashion:

> During a prayer-meeting some of these fashionables were grouped together, singing a hymn which was very popular in

[37] Posey, *Frontier Mission*, 25.
[38] C. A. Johnson, *Frontier Camp Meeting*, 210.

HISTORY OF COSMOPOLITE;

OR

THE FOUR VOLUMES OF

LORENZO DOW'S JOURNAL

CONCENTRATED IN ONE,

CONTAINING HIS

EXPERIENCE AND TRAVELS,

FROM CHILDHOOD TO NEAR HIS FIFTIETH YEAR.

ALSO HIS

POLEMICAL WRITINGS;

CONSISTING OF

I. HIS CHAIN, WITH FIVE LINKS, TWO HOOKS AND A SWIVEL.
II. REFLECTIONS ON MATRIMONY.
III. ANALECTS UPON THE RIGHTS OF MAN.
IV. A JOURNEY FROM BABYLON TO JERUSALEM.
V. DIALOGUE BETWEEN THE CURIOUS AND SINGULAR.
VI. HINTS ON THE FULFILMENT OF PROPHECY.
VII. ON CHURCH GOVERNMENT AND THE MINISTRY, &C. &C.

TO WHICH IS ADDED

THE "JOURNEY OF LIFE," BY PEGGY DOW

FIFTH EDITION.

REVISED AND CORRECTED, WITH NOTES

PUBLISHED BY JOSHUA MARTIN.
PRINTED BY JOHN B. WOLFF, WHEELING, VA.
1848.

Title page for a Southern printing of Lorenzo Dow, *History of Cosmopolite* (Wheeling, Va., 1848). Photographed from a copy deposited in the University of California, Berkeley, Library.

those days. This hymn, the chorus of which was

> "I want to get to heaven
> My long sought rest,"

they sang with great animation, and their animation increased as they saw the presiding elder advance and join them. It was discovered after a while that he changed the last line of the chorus, and instead of singing,

> "I want to get to heaven
> My long sought rest,"

he sang,

> "I want to get to heaven
> With my long short dress." [39]

But the good times of the camp-meeting were sometimes less innocuous. Liquor dispensers and prostitutes often attended, and it has been suggested that "some of the women who were the most persistent victims of the 'falling exercise' were the ones prone to forget the edict of virtue." [40] The camp-meeting was also a perfect site for the bullying activities of local ruffians, who were usually present in force. By and large, however, the good accomplished by the meetings was more than sufficient in the eyes of religious leaders to cancel out any harmful effects that the practice, in its social aspects, might have carried with it.

Yet, in spite of their great success, camp-meetings virtually disappeared in the 1840s. In part, their discontinuance may have been because of the fact that increasing population density in many areas made the establishment of "located" churches feasible so that it was no longer necessary to draw people from over a large area in order to make a religious meeting worthwhile. A good-sized congregation could be attracted from the immediate neighborhood. But the disappearance of the camp-meeting was just as likely a product of larger historical and social forces, for it paralleled other significant changes in both the Methodist and Baptist churches. Both groups were changing status from that of sects offering alternatives to the status quo to that of denominational institutions within the existing Southern social order.

[39] Strickland, *Jacob Gruber*, 79.
[40] C. A. Johnson, *Frontier Camp Meeting*, 54.

Several significant developments in Methodist and Baptist practices signaled the alteration in status. For one, both groups came to rely less on uneducated or self-educated, divinely called frontier preachers and more on a seminary-trained, settled clergy, and in the 1830s both Methodists and Baptists set about founding colleges in the South and West. The change was more than superficially important because it meant that no longer did one have to receive direct divine inspiration in order to be fit for the ministry. Instead, one could be trained in the world for the job. Old itinerants such as Peter Cartwright saw in this the potential secularization of the clergy; the itinerants knew that a generation of educated men would be unable to comprehend the profundity of frontier religious experience, and they were right. The new-style clergy founded theological journals to debate, among other matters, the merits of the revival method, carrying on such debates in remarkably abstract terms—ignoring, specifically, the question of efficacy. As a result, according to Cartwright, when one of these trained ministers confronted a fallen sinner, the best exhortation he could come up with was, "Be composed; be composed."[41]

At the same time, there was a growing affluence among both Methodists and Baptists. Not that most church-folk became planters, for the majority remained outside the mainstream of the Southern system. Still, because enough of the church-folk did achieve worldly success, by the 1840s Methodism had overtaken Episcopalianism as the slaveowners' church, with the Baptists running a close second.[42]

Growing affluence was accompanied by a changing morality, especially in regard to Methodist and Baptist views on the issue of slavery. At the opening of the nineteenth century, both groups were on record as opposing the institution. When the Methodist Episcopal church was formed as an independent body in 1784, a rule was adopted through the force of John Wesley and the American leaders Francis Asbury and Thomas Coke requiring every

---

[41] Cartwright, *Autobiography*, 81, 371.
[42] Walter Brownlow Posey, *The Baptist Church in the Lower Mississippi Valley, 1776–1845*, 89.

slaveowning member to emancipate his slaves within one year.[43] To some itinerants, such as Peter Cartwright, slavery was always an evil to preach against, and he ultimately left the South rather than succumb to pressures to stay away from the topic. Others, like Jacob Gruber, even found themselves temporarily afoul of the law for their protestations against the South's evil.[44] Baptists, with their local organization, never took such a united stand, but in the years around 1800 several Southern congregations declared slavery to be contrary to their religion.[45] Nevertheless, as both organizations began to grow in the South their opposition to slavery steadily decreased. Growing Southern paranoia led to trouble for the more ardent antislavery preachers, and many had to leave the South. By 1845 Southern churchmen of both denominations had completely reversed the position of their forebears. During the years 1844 and 1845 both Southern Methodists and Southern Baptists left their Northern brethren over the slavery issue. It is especially significant that the immediate stimulus for the Methodists was a debate over whether the same man could be both a bishop and a planter at the same time.

These changes, and others, marked the shift in Methodist and Baptist status from sects concerned with the frontier folk at the margins of Southern society to denominations contributing to the very fabric of the social order. Spiritual experience and concomitant exclusivity lost their central place. The leadership, now educated, was no longer of the frontier folk but of professionals, and it was growing in affluence. In addition, the morality was no longer an alternative set of standards but a duplicate set of Southern society in general. Liston Pope, discussing modern Southern sectarianism, has outlined the process. As the sect begins to grow, it reaches out for more influence. Regardless of its original stance in opposition to much of the social order, the sect begins to prize

---

[43] Posey, *The Development of Methodism in the Old Southwest, 1783–1824*, 95.

[44] Strickland, *Jacob Gruber*, 140. The best and most thorough study of the problem of slavery for the Methodist church is, of course, Donald G. Mathews, *Slavery and Methodism*, esp. chs. 2 and 9.

[45] John Lee Eighmy, *Churches in Cultural Captivity*, 4–5.

converts from the elite or to prize the achievement of high status among its members. In the process the sect begins to accommodate to the culture from which it had originally withdrawn, for only by such accommodation can it continue to expand its scope of influence. All the members need not have achieved material success for the group to lose its identification with those at the margins of society. It need only be the case that *some* members succeed for prosperity and influence to become the guiding lights of church practice.[46]

As some Methodists and Baptists became more affluent and more "responsible," sectarian practices such as those of the camp-meeting were no longer thought appropriate. There is little "responsible" or "respectable" in the cries of a fallen sinner. It is better for all concerned that the sinner "be composed"; if he be anguished, let him keep his anguish to himself. The denominations were no longer concerned with providing an alternative world and an alternative life because their leaders and many of their members had succeeded in terms of the world as it was.

The same impulse which led to camp-meetings led to their demise. The practice was begun in order to increase the outreach of the sects, and it succeeded admirably; but that same evangelistic outreach could not be promoted by a practice which belonged only to the marginal folk of the frontier. Evangelism dictated that the church broaden its social base if it were to continue to grow, and the camp-meeting was too much a part of the frontier church-folk to satisfy such a dictate. The denominations, unlike the sects, did not belong to the plain-folk, but to Southern society in general.

The Methodists and Baptists were most attuned to the needs of frontier society during the sectarian period of their development. Although their protest morality and disciplines created a new arena in which the frontier church-folk could find some degree of stability and relief from the tensions of daily life, the social role of the sects was only half the story. Most people undoubtedly went into the churches for religious reasons—they felt they had actually been converted by the power of God. They may

[46] Liston Pope, *Millhands and Preachers*, 119.

have welcomed the stability achieved through the disciplines, but they were more concerned for their souls than for their society. If one is fully to understand the appeal of the frontier sects, one must be able to say something about the sort of religion their members espoused.

In the camp-meeting, again, the plain-folk were able to proclaim their religion. Originating on the frontier, the practice was not imposed on the people either as a product of their European Protestant heritage or by some governing body foreign to them. In fact, the practice never was institutionalized by the Methodist hierarchy, nor did it meet with universal Baptist approval. Further, the clergy who administered the meetings were themselves of the plain-folk, or considered themselves to be. Its association with the frontier folk was so complete that when the churches ceased to be devoted to that group, the camp-meeting ceased to play a significant role in church practice.

At the same time it was a good deal more than a major social event. While the camp-meeting may have appealed to some people as a kind of "holy fair," there were too many other social occasions on the frontier for that to be a sufficient explanation of the growth and development of the practice. Instead, its popularity was the result of the unique way in which the camp-meeting satisfied the religious needs of the people of the frontier. Everything that went on in a camp-meeting was of the plain-folk's devising and grew out of a response to their needs, not only in the practice of camping out as an answer to the frontier environment, but also in the very structure of the meeting and in the words that were spoken or sung. The camp-meeting was, in other words, the clearest expression of what was felt and believed by frontier Baptists and Methodists, and, as such, is the best place to look for an understanding of what religion meant to them.

III

TO GIVE OLD SATAN ANOTHER ROUND

The Camp-Meeting

FROM THE POINT OF VIEW of the leaders of frontier religion, the only reason for holding camp-meetings was to convert new church members. Any other functions the meetings might have performed for frontier society in general or for the sects in particular were subordinate to this one major aim. When camp-meetings were discussed and evaluated by preachers and sectarian leaders, the talk focused on the efficacy of the meetings for converting new members, and particular meetings were judged successful or unsuccessful solely on the basis of how many new souls were brought to God and the church. The same criterion, the number of converts, gave the camp-meeting preachers an objective yardstick by which to measure their skills. Central to the gathering, then, was the bringing on of conversions among those in attendance, and all the activities of the camp-meeting were set to that end.

Religious experience is, of course, an intensely personal matter, and experiences of divine power can take many forms, from the vivid visions of mystics to a less spectacular but no less real inner feeling of peace and strength. Nevertheless, for the frontier sects, as for most conversionist religious groups, not just any experience would do. The would-be church member had to give an account of his conversion before those who were already part of the group, and the account he gave had to ring true to his auditors. There were acceptable conversions, and there were those which were

A camp-meeting, frontispiece to B. W. Gorham, *Camp Meeting Manual* (Boston, 1854). Photographed from a copy deposited in the Kansas State University Library.

not so acceptable: the frontier sects were not without their share of false prophets. Thus, it was not enough that the camp-meetings effect conversions; it was also important that the conversions be of the proper sort.

The correct form for conversion among white frontier church-folk was set down in no uncertain terms in the biographies and autobiographies of the most vigorous practitioners of frontier religion, the preachers. Although most of these biographies and autobiographies were written in the quarter century following the heyday of the camp-meeting,[1] they were more than exercises in nostalgia. In their accounts, or in the accounts written by devoted followers, the preachers were setting down for all time a way of

[1] Louis Kaplan, compiler, in association with James Tyler Cook, Clinton E. Colby, Jr., and Daniel C. Haskell, *A Bibliography of American Autobiographies.*

life which had meant much to them. Their writings were testimonials to the meaning of religion in the life of an individual, and for each of the preachers such meaning had been derived from the central fact of having experienced the converting grace of the divine. As individuals, of course, their lives varied enormously, but the basic focus for each came out of that central experience, and the morphology of conversion they recounted showed no variation from individual to individual.[2] One began his life as a sinner and remained in that awful condition until he experienced the saving power of the Lord. From that time until his death, he was to live in the service of the divine and the church, carried on by an assurance that an eternal life in heaven awaited him after death. This form for conversion, as elaborated on the Southern frontier, was at the basis of the camp-meeting and of the religious beliefs of the Southern church-folk.

The preconversion lives of the preachers were invariably "worldly" and sinful. Methodist itinerant Peter Cartwright described his younger years in a way that was a virtual catalogue of church-folk vice: "I was naturally a wild, wicked boy, and delighted in horse-racing, card-playing, and dancing."[3] Of the early life of a Virginia Baptist, Jeremiah Vardeman, it was said, "His duty to God was wholly neglected, and he lived after the course of the world. . . . Conviction of his sin and folly often drove him back to sinful pleasures for temporary relief." Yet the pleasure was not unqualified. At the same time that the sinful young men pursued their wicked ways, there were pressures on them to turn toward God. While Vardeman, for example, tried to make his escape into the wicked life of the world, his mother "clung to him with a mother's love, strengthened by faith in the Divine promises, and in the power and grace of the Lord Jesus Christ. . . . 'I know Jerry will be reclaimed. God is faithful, and I feel assured he is a

---

[2] The religious autobiography as a model for conversion has a long tradition in Anglo-America. See Daniel B. Shea, *Spiritual Autobiography in Early America*, 100. See also Edmund S. Morgan, *Visible Saints*, 66. For the English background to the tradition see William Haller, *The Rise of Puritanism*, 90–111.

[3] Cartwright, *Autobiography*, 27.

prayer-hearing God.' "[4] Certainly, learning about the righteous way was a part of growing up for many children on the frontier. The Pennsylvania Baptist Jacob Bower remembered:

> My parents belonged to the denomination of Christians called Tunkers, as early as I can recollect my Father kept up regular morning and eavning worship in the family. Commonly he would read a chapter in the German Testament, then sing a hymn in German, then say a prayer in the same language, and were taught to sing with them. We were instructed such lessons as we were able to understand, such as this. Be good children, all good children when they die will go to a good place, wher Jesus is, and many pretty Angels, and they would be happy forever. Bad children when they die will go to a bad place, where there is a great fire and the Devil and his Angels tormenting the wicked forever.[5]

The main effect of these two simultaneous influences was to set up a tension between the kind of life which the frontier youths liked to lead and the feelings about that life which those most responsible for their upbringing, usually their mothers, attempted to instill. As Cartwright expressed such a tension: "My father restrained me but little, though my mother often talked to me, wept over me, and prayed for me, and often drew tears from my eyes; and though I often wept under preaching and resolved to do better and seek religion, yet I broke my vows, went into young company, rode races, played cards, and danced."[6] The life of the world continued for Cartwright and Vardeman, as for others, despite their mothers' desire that they turn to religion. It was not simply that they felt guilty, although, as Cartwright shows, they did. It was more that the religious influence instilled in them a sense that all was not right with the worldly way of life which the young men led. Thus the seed was implanted: the first step in the conversion process grew out of that feeling.

"Conviction" came when the tension between one's worldly

---

[4] William B. Sprague, *Baptists*, 420.
[5] In Sweet, I, *Baptists*, 186.
[6] Cartwright, *Autobiography*, 27.

life and religion could no longer be borne, the religious life having been acknowledged as immensely superior. The life of the world was completely rejected, an event usually spurred by one's witnessing of death and disaster or by coming under preaching. The case of Jacob Bower was not unusual.

> Soon we met large companies of Negro-s, we passed several companies, at length we met an old man walking by himself, I stopped him and enquired of him, where they were all going so early this morning. The old negro said, "we are all going to Beards Town [Kentucky] to see a fellow servant hung to day for killing his fellow servant." I started on with this thought, how does that man feal, knowing that he must die to day. Suddenly as if some one had asked me. And how do you feal? You don't know but that you may die before he does. All of a sudden, (ah I shall never forget it) as if a book had been opened to me, the inside of which I had never seen: I got a sight of the wretchedness of my heart—a cage of every unclean and hateful thing. (ah thought I, here lies the root of bitterness, the fountain from which all my sinful actions have flowed. My mind & heart have always been enmity against God, who is so holy that he cannot allow of no sin, however small it may appear in the sight of men. How can I ever be admitted into Heaven with such a heart? it is uterly imposible. Lost, lost forever lost.[7]

This was only the beginning of Bower's conviction, for he was one who suffered through the great earthquake which struck the upper South in the second decade of the nineteenth century, an event which, not surprisingly, brought many to grace. A few days after his stirrings on the road, Bower was subject to the "follish thought . . . that I must not give up to God to do with me as he pleased, for I thought that the moment that I did that, he would kill me and send me instantly to hell." He was even afraid to sleep "for fear that if I went to sleep, I would awake in hell."[8] The profound symbolism of the surrounding cracks in the earth was not lost on Bower.

[7] Sweet, I, *Baptists*, 190.
[8] Ibid., 192–93.

In the case of Jacob Young, a mere suggestion made at a camp-meeting did the trick.

> An aged minister by the name of Daniel Woodfield preached. The circuit preacher exhorted, and a glorious display of Divine power followed. The congregation was melted into tears. . . . I became very uneasy, and changed my position; while standing on my feet, a pious man approached me and addressed me in the following words: "Jacob Young, I suppose this appears to be enthusiasm to you." I attempted to reply, but had lost the power of speech—my tears flowed freely, my knees became feeble, and I trembled like Belshazzar.[9]

The emotional rejection of preconversion life, either in the characterization of that life as "unclean and hateful," as in the case of Bower, or hypocritical, as with Young, was accompanied by a rejection and renunciation of worldly friends. Lorenzo Dow, echoing the prophet Jeremiah, said, "I at once broke off from my old companions and evil practices, which some call innocent mirth. . . . Soon I became like a great speckled bird, among the birds of the forest, in the eyes of my friends."[10]

Separation from one's former life was to have been complete, both physically and emotionally. Yet, it was not a separation *into* a new life, as Bower's account makes quite clear: he felt "lost, lost forever lost." Not only was the convicted sinner separated from all he had known, but he felt he had no place to go, for, like Bower, he was still apart from God as well. He remained damned, but under conviction; he felt his damnation with great intensity. Dow wrote that, "striving to pray, I felt as if the heavens were brass and the earth iron; it seemed as though my prayers did not go higher than my head."[11]

Conviction was followed by the actual experience of conversion. As the descriptions of conviction show, the individual recognized his inability to convert himself, acknowledging that he had to rely on the mercy and power of the divine to let him know

---

9 Young, *Autobiography*, 41.
10 Dow, *The Dealings of God, Man, and the Devil*, 11.
11 Ibid., 12.

that his past sins were forgiven so that he could be certain of a place in heaven. This could happen shortly after conviction, or after weeks and weeks, or, as in the case of Lorenzo Dow, after several years. Jacob Bower's ordeal is illuminating.

> For several days past, I had been thinking about giving up to God and resign myself into his hands for I can do nothing to save myself, and all I do is so sinful in his sight that he disregards my cries & prayers. . . .
>
> The more I tryed to pray, the less hope I had of being Saved. Just about midnight I was sittin in a chair, absorbed in deep thought about my condition—I well recollect thinking, Oh how much do I suffer in this world. . . . Suddenly my thoughts turned to the sufferings of Christ and what he endured on the cross. That he suffered in soul & body, his soul was exceeding sorrowful even unto death, sweting as it had been great drops of blood falling to the ground; and all his painful sufferings for the space of three hours on the cross, and that not for himself; it was for sinners that he thus suffered that they mite be saved. . . . If it was done for sinners, it was done for me.[12]

Jacob Young lay on the floor many hours, his soul "dark," until at last "the light" appeared, and he was "translated from the power of darkness into the kingdom of God's dear Son."[13]

With conversion, the tension of conviction was resolved through the intervention of the divine. One can recall Jacob Young's utter impotence at the moment of conviction: accused of irreligion, he could make no reply. Subsequently, his incapacity grew so great that he lay on the floor in a trance for several hours. While he was thus helpless, "the light appeared," and he was converted. For Bower the moment came when he had completely given himself up, though not to the extent which Young had. When one achieved a state of complete alienation from the past and the divine, and from oneself, it became possible for the divine to intervene to effect conversion. A Methodist preacher, John Hagerty, has briefly described the resulting state of "assurance" in a letter:

[12] Sweet, I, *Baptists*, 192–93.
[13] Young, *Autobiography*, 42.

When I was on my knees crying to God for a full Deliverance I heard a voice inwardly say, "I have sealed the pardon of thy sins with my blood." I felt the truth of it in my heart and in a moment prayer was turned into praise. I wanted all the world to help me praise my God. In a few moments I fell prostrate before the Lord [and] determined not [to] rise untill I knew the Lord had pardoned me and in a little while the same words were imprest on my mind more strongly than before. I was more assured of his forgiving love and enjoyed much peace in believing I now thought I never should sin more. My mind was taken up with God, and I convers'd with Him as a Man with his Friend. My confidence was unshaken and my hope full of immortality.[14]

The state of assurance contrasted sharply with the condition of one under conviction. The sinner's wretchedness and uncleanness were quite the opposite of the peace of the forgiven convert who believed he "never should sin more." Conversing with God "as a Man with his Friend" is a change for one formerly afraid of a God who might kill him and send him instantly to hell. And a hope of immortality came to replace that fear of death which was often a critical stimulus to the onset of conviction.

The first component in the conversion experience, then, was an individual's preconversion life whose main features—worldly sinful behavior and the presence of a strong religious influence—created a tension between two irreconcilable paths of life, the worldly and the religious. The second component, and the first step in the actual conversion process, was conviction, involving a separation from the life of the world, usually emphasized by a separation from the people who had been one's companions in that life and based on an acknowledgment of the world's wretchedness. Simultaneously there came to the sinner a knowledge of his own uncleanness and, hence, his unworthiness for a religious life. The potential convert was no longer what he had been, but neither was he what he hoped to become.

This period of ambiguity constituted the most important aspect of the conversion experience, for it was a period when the struc-

[14] In Sweet, IV, *Methodists*, 126. Brackets in Sweet.

tural framework of an individual's life was negated as he passed from one state or condition to another. Yet it was precisely during the unstructured period that the individual was enabled to come into contact with the divine. Prior to conversion the individual's life had had a certain order to it, but the order was all wrong because it was based upon participation in worldly activities. The goals which one wished to attain were worldly goals, just as one's friends had been fellow sinners, and they blocked the way to God. Only through the negation of that order, and of any order of human devising, could one hope to come into contact with the divine and to achieve the state of assurance which was to be desired above all else. The state of assurance—the knowledge that one had, indeed, found the way to God—put the individual in a new relationship with the things of this world, placing those things in an order devised by the divine. But such a new order could be imposed only after the thoroughgoing displacement of the old.[15]

The accounts of conversion which appear in the preacher autobiographies follow a set form and have but minor variations in specifics. In following this form, the message of the accounts seems to be more than the story of how conversion happened for one individual: the autobiographies were exemplary, setting forth the proper form for conversion. The morphology of religious experience outlined in the autobiographies was a description of the way in which interaction between man and God was supposed to occur.

Because there was a proper form for conversion, those experiences which were the goal of the camp-meeting had to be effected in that form. The preachers did not want something—anything—to happen to the convert. Rather, they wanted a particular kind of interaction to occur between the individual and the divine. The form of the camp-meeting ensured this, for it was a collective ex-

---

[15] The conversion experience is interpreted here as a kind of rite of passage in the life of an individual, an interpretation based on the structure outlined in Arnold van Gennep, *The Rites of Passage*, esp. 11; and in Victor W. Turner, "Betwixt and Between: The Liminal Period in *Rites de Passage*," in June Helm, ed., *Symposium on New Approaches in the Study of Religion* (Proceedings of the American Ethnological Society, 1964), esp. 8.

pression of the pattern of conversion which the preachers had set down: in its components, the meeting paralleled the morphology of the preachers' individual conversions, but it made the experience available to an exceedingly large number of people. To see how this was so, it will be necessary to examine camp-meeting activities in more detail.

In most areas, camp-meetings were held annually at harvest time, although they could take place throughout the warm season. Published reports from itinerants as well as newspaper announcements show that dates ranged from July until October, but by far the greatest number was in late September. The timing was important, since the fall date made it easy for plain-folk to spend several days away from home and the burdens of farming, thus enabling the greatest number of people to attend.

The choice of a site was also important and was based on several factors. Northern Methodist B. W. Gorham gave three criteria which seem to have applied in the South as well. First, the encampment should be held in a hospitable neighborhood, preferably for Gorham one populated by Methodists, because among the problems which plagued campers was frequent disruption of proceedings by drunken outsiders, as well as exploitation by prostitutes and vendors of the wrong kind of spiritual refreshment. One way to cut down on those problems was to locate the meeting in an area where the surrounding community was thoroughly on the side of religion. Second, necessary requirements for a site were adequate natural resources of water and pasture land to support a crowd in the thousands, many of whom had come from too far away to bring their provisions along.[16] Some reports say that campers came from an area with a radius of up to one hundred miles,[17] but as the country grew more populous, fifty miles was a more usual distance. Even this, of course, made the campers' homes inaccessible, and as the contemporary writer James Hall noted, "it took a *powerful chance* of truck, to feed such a *heap of*

---

[16] B. W. Gorham, *Camp Meeting Manual*, 121.
[17] See, for example, a "Letter from a Gentleman to His Sister in Philadelphia, dated Lexington, Kentucky, August 10, 1801," in Sweet, I, *Baptists*, 610.

folks."[18] Third, a somewhat less tangible though no less important criterion for a site was its suitability as a place which conveyed
the proper camp-meeting atmosphere when cleared—when the
small trees were removed, the large ones remaining should form
a natural canopy of tree limbs over the site, the effect being to
emphasize the site in contrast to the natural gloom of the forest
and to create a cathedral in the wilderness.

Although camp sites could be of several possible shapes—
horseshoe shaped, circular, or rectangular—certain internal elements were always present. The main feature, by all accounts,
was the preachers' stand or pulpit, the floor of which was elevated
from 5 to 6½ feet above the ground. Immediately in front of the

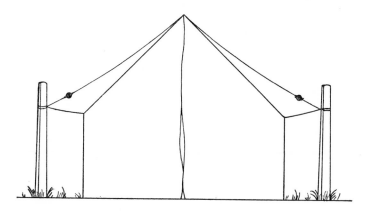

Model for a tent (12 ft. wide),
from B. W. Gorham, *Camp Meeting Manual.*

stand was an area variously known as the altar, mourners' bench, or
anxious seat. Unsympathetic observers called the area "the glory
pen," and in spite of the derogatory connotations, this provided
an accurate description; for, although there were sometimes seats
in the pen, its significance was as a distinct area, separated from
the congregation and the pulpit, where sinners under conviction

[18] James Hall, *Legends of the West,* 9. Italics in the original.

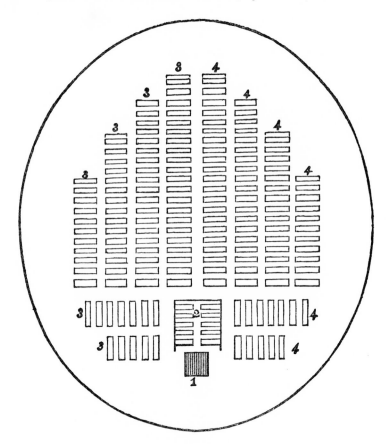

LEGEND:

1. Stand, or speakers' platform.
2. Altar.
3. Seats—ladies' side.
4. Seats—gentlemen's side.
C. Circle on the outside of which the tents are to be built.

Campground plan, from B. W. Gorham, *Camp Meeting Manual*. Photographed from a copy deposited in the Kansas State University Library.

were brought to experience conversion. Beyond the pen were two sections of seats made of stumps or planks for the congregation.

In the site plan several distinctions were made among the camp-meeting participants. White men were kept separate from white women either by a center aisle separating the seats into two sections, or, on occasion, by a rail fence between the two sections. White worshipers were kept apart from black, the whites sitting in front of the stand with the blacks gathering at the back. Finally, the elevation of the pulpit put the preachers above everyone else, and when they were not preaching, the ministers were kept still farther apart, since permanent living quarters were maintained for them within or above the pulpit itself.[19]

According to their roles, there were several kinds of participants in a camp-meeting. The divinities who influenced the success of a particular gathering were, of course, indispensable. Success depended not so much on the participation of the supernatural entities themselves as upon manifestations of their power, sometimes described indirectly in such phrases as "divine light" or "heavenly fire," but more commonly attributed directly to God. James Finley, a Methodist itinerant, recounted on the singing of a spiritual by the Reverend Robert Manley at a camp-meeting in Ohio: "Before he had finished singing the fourth verse, the *power of God* came down, and pervaded the vast assembly, and it became agitated—swelling and surging like the sea in a storm."[20] The power of God was usually associated, as it was in this statement, with the degree to which members of the congregation were affected by the activities of the clergy. A. P. Mead, in his camp-meeting manual, showed another similar but more common attitude toward the role of the power of God in a meeting in his account of an exhortation delivered at a Kentucky camp-meeting in 1801:

> [A young boy] spoke for near an hour with that convincing eloquence that could be inspired only from heaven; and when

[19] C. A. Johnson, *Frontier Camp Meeting*, 46; Gorham, *Camp Meeting Manual*, 128–29.

[20] James B. Finley, *Autobiography of Rev. James B. Finley*, 228.

exhausted, and language failed to describe the feelings of his soul, he raised his handkerchief and dropping it, cried, "Thus, O sinner, will you drop into hell unless you forsake your sins and turn to God." At this moment, the power of God fell upon the assembly, and sinners fell like men slain in mighty battle, and the cries for mercy seemed as though they would rend the mighty heavens.[21]

In Mead's account, the power of God was responsible for both the eloquence of the youthful exhorter and the onset of those religious exercises which were so much a part of the camp-meeting. Most of the ministers, in fact, defended the camp-meeting from charges of "enthusiasm" on the ground that the activities being criticized, chiefly the physical exercises, were manifestations of the power of God rather than extravagances on the part of the faithful.

The power of God had to be present for a meeting to be successful, but many of the activities in the camp-meeting were directed to the Lord Jesus. The people addressed Jesus in several ways, including exhortations and songs, but the role of Jesus in the meeting was shown most clearly in the cries of convicted sinners: "Jesus! Jesus!" "Come down, Lord Jesus!" and so on. Although both the power of God and the activities of Jesus were essential to a successful meeting, there was a difference in their roles. The power of God seems never to have been directly invoked; man could take no initiative in bringing that power to earth. Jesus' presence, on the other hand, could be invoked. Further, Jesus' activities were part of a specific portion of the camp-meeting—the conversion of sinners—whereas the power of God was assigned responsibility for the overall quality of the camp-meeting.

The insiders at a camp-meeting were those who had experienced conversion. Some of them played an active role in leading the camp-meeting proceedings, while others participated as members of the congregation. Preachers, white exhorters, and black exhorters were the professional leaders of the camp-meeting. The preachers were ordained clergymen who delivered sermons. The

[21] A. P. Mead, *Manna in the Wilderness*, 22.

white exhorters were also ordained clergymen whose chief duty was inviting sinners to enter the pen by reminding them of the prospects of hell and damnation awaiting those who failed to take the step. The position of exhorter was an official one in the Methodist organization, occupied by a young man who aspired to be an itinerant; as an exhorter, one exercised his gifts before a local congregation or assisted a circuit rider for a year.[22] In many camp-meeting services, however, this position was filled by one of the regular ministers, equal in status to the preacher:

> We were both to preach in succession, commencing at eleven o'clock. He was to preach first, and I to follow. Said he to me:
> "If I strike fire, I will immediately call for mourners, and you must go into the assembly and exhort in every direction, and I will manage the altar. But," said he, "if I fail to strike fire, you must preach; and if you strike fire, call the mourners and manage the altar. I will go through the congregation, and exhort with all the power God gives me."[23]

The duties of the black exhorter were identical to those of his white counterpart, and apparently black exhorters had some degree of professional status. However, they usually faced the black audience in back of the stand, and did not often direct their efforts toward the white congregation.

Among nonprofessional leaders were lay preachers especially invited to deliver a sermon, convert exhorters, and "good singers and praying persons."[24] Two accounts of camp-meetings written by travelers to the South report principal sermons at morning services delivered by attorneys living in the neighborhood of the meetings.[25] In each case the sermon was described as having been "ethical" in content, and the role of the scheduled lay preacher was identical to that of an ordained clergyman. The convert exhorters, unlike their professional counterparts, appeared somewhat

[22] C. A. Johnson, *Frontier Camp Meeting*, 20.
[23] Cartwright, *Autobiography*, 120.
[24] Ibid., 353.
[25] Fredrika Bremer, *The Homes of the New World: Impressions of America*, 2 vols., I, 314; James Flint, *Letters from America, 1818–1820*, 266.

spontaneously at two points during the camp-meeting. Often, during that period when people were being converted, new converts would move among convicted sinners, exhorting them to "come to Jesus." Whereas the professional exhorters, like all the sectarian leadership, were men, convert exhorters were often women and children, as in the following incident.

> At Indian Creek [Kentucky] a boy from appearance about twelve years of age, retired from the stand in time of preaching, under a very extraordinary impression; and having mounted a log at some distance, and raising his voice in a very affecting manner; he attracted the main body of the people in a very few minutes. With tears streaming from his eyes, he cried aloud to the wicked, warning them of their danger, denouncing their certain doom if they persisted in their sins; expressing his love to their souls, and desire that they would turn to the Lord be saved.[26]

Exhorting as new converts was one of the few activities in which women could assume an important role in the functioning of the frontier sects. Generally, their position in frontier religious organizations was analogous to their place in frontier society. The major operations of the churches were dominated by men, who had all the ecclesiastical authority. Only at the height of excitement in a camp-meeting could women come to share in the leadership of frontier religious activities. New converts also appeared during morning services to recount the events of their own conversions. In such testimonials, as they were called, the new converts would describe the joys of assurance, contrasting their new condition with their prior wretchedness as sinners. Those who testified during scheduled services, as opposed to those who appeared spontaneously, were almost always men.

A final group of leaders was composed of "good singers and praying persons" whose chief duty was the "recovery" of those who had fallen under the power of God. As the exercises associated

---

[26] "Theophilus Armenius" [sic], "Account of the Rise and Progress of the Work of God in the Western Country," *Methodist Magazine* 2 (1819), 224. This may be an earlier version of the story told by A. P. Mead and quoted on pp. 73–74 above.

with conversion appeared, affected individuals were surrounded by good singers and praying persons for encouragement. Convicted sinners who were in trances were taken into tents to be recovered by members of this group.

Many people who took part in the camp-meeting did so without assuming any kind of leadership role, but they were still church members who had undergone conversion. They referred to themselves in terms which indicated both their solidarity and their special status, using expressions which have had a long currency among sectarian Christians. They addressed each other as "Brother" and "Sister," and thought of themselves, collectively, as "Brethren" —all terms which had been used by the earliest Christians.[27] Other expressions drew on the sectarian tradition as well as that of the early church. The people spoke of themselves as a community of "saints" and as "soldiers" engaged in a spiritual warfare, thus identifying themselves as a unified group, standing on their faith and feeling apart from the sins of the world.

Those converted at the meeting were, at one time or another, sinners, mourners, or converts. The terms do not refer to different groups so much as to a single group of people moving through the different stages of conversion. The efforts of the camp-meeting exhorters were aimed at the sinners—those who were not church members and who were, therefore, leading the life of the world. The sinners' condition was like the preconversion conditions of the preachers, and the vivid imagery of the exhortations served to remind them of their distance from God. As one exhorter told them, "Go, sinner; go to hell and be ruined forever, and I will say, amen! Go on, if you want to, after all that has been done for you by a dying Saviour and a living ministry."[28] By means of such appeals, exhorters hoped to bring outsiders under conviction, thus starting sinners on the road to conversion.

Mourners were those sinners who had become convicted and were "mourning" for the doom which appeared inevitable. They were also called "anxious" or "penitent," words which have about

[27] Hall, *Legends*, 10.
[28] In Mead, *Manna*, 56.

the same connotations. In the context of the camp-meeting, mourners were in that transitional state between the life of a sinner and the new life of a convert, and they were also the people who were going through the physical exercises.

After a period of "wrestling and praying" during which they were physically exercised, mourners were converted. The conversion thus accomplished was considered to be complete, as the English churchmen Reed and Matheson pointed out critically:

> And in many instances, especially among the Methodist denomination, the anxious seat or the altar, and the acts of rising or kneeling, are in reality, if not with formal design, made terms of state. They are used, too, not only to express the reality of awakened concern; but as tests of having "submitted to Christ," "found hope," and of being "true converts."[29]

Although the three categories were used to refer to essentially the same group, "sinners" was a more inclusive term, describing all who had not undergone conversion. "Mourners" was somewhat more exclusive, including only those sinners who had been awakened and convicted. "Converts" were those mourners who had made the transition and had been converted by the Lord. In theory, not all mourners were converted, but in practice it appears that once one had gone so far as to mourn for one's fate, he would likely be converted.

One other group of converts must be noted, for not all of those who underwent conversion at a camp-meeting were doing so for the first time. Mrs. Trollope, a most unfriendly observer, reports an exhortation in which a young convert cried, "Woe! woe to backsliders! hear it, hear it Jesus! when I was fifteen my mother died, and I backslided, oh Jesus, I backslided! take me home to my mother, Jesus!"[30] When one backslid, he fell away from the church and returned to the ways of the world. Many cases of backsliders returning home were recorded in the preacher autobiographies. Therefore, it is likely that many of those converted

---

[29] Reed and Matheson, *Visit to the American Churches*, II, 34.
[30] Frances Trollope, *Domestic Manners of the Americans*, 2 vols., I, 240.

at a camp-meeting were not new to the church but rather were old members who needed a renewal of their faith. In fact, it was not unusual for camp-meetings to be held in areas where the population was thought by the church leaders to have slipped into infidelity, for the express purpose of bringing the backsliders back to the faith. Finally, although initiates—whether for the first time or for a renewal of experience—included both males and females of all ages, in the words of one observer, "This species of infatuation happens chiefly among the women."[31]

In travelers' accounts, outsiders had little or no function in the conduct of camp-meetings, but to participant-reporters, outsiders were of great importance either as sinners and potential converts or as subversive and even disruptive agents. The travelers who wrote accounts of camp-meetings were, of course, one kind of outsider and were in a class with those others who came to watch, to meet friends and socialize, to politic, or to make honest money. The insiders noticed such people only when they got in the way of those desiring to participate actively. Somewhat worse were the religious opponents of the camp-meeting, the "dry old professors" and Calvinists, particularly some antimission Baptist preachers. To itinerants, these opponents were tools of Satan, and they delighted in telling stories in their autobiographies of how Calvinists were not merely defeated in open debate but were even converted to Methodism.

At the extreme were the mockers and scoffers, thought to be agents of the devil, who heckled the believers, broke camp rules, and even tried to beat up preachers. The hecklers too were often defeated by the power of God working through the preachers, and thus were converted and reformed, further attesting to the great strength of camp-meeting religion. Another frequent result of the taunts of the hecklers was the unification of the church-folk in the common goal of thwarting the threats posed by such disruptive elements.

Much of the activity of camp-meeting has been described in

---

[31] François André Michaux, *Travels West of the Allegheny Mountains, 1802*, 249.

the identification of participants, for one's identity was based upon what one did in the context of the meeting rather than upon who one was at other times. Generally speaking, the only difference between a preacher and an exhorter, for example, lay in what each did, and not in who he was. But it is now necessary to look more closely at the sequence of events in the camp-meeting. Although there was certainly no such thing as an archetypal camp-meeting, certain elements appear to have occurred in a common pattern at most gatherings.

Prior to the opening services of any camp-meeting the participants assembled at the encampment, the place and date having been announced in newspapers and on handbills several months in advance. As the congregation gathered, the campers set up their tents and renewed acquaintances. For the brethren, this involved "the interchange of apostolic greetings and embraces, and talk of the coming solemnities."[32] For the clergy it was a time to invoke divine aid that they might have success:

> "Have you everything you need?"
> "I have not. The most important article is yet to be put up."
> "What can it be?"
> "My sword, of course. A soldier without his sword is poorly fitted for battle."
> Will a minister of Jesus presume to take an instrument of death to camp meeting? Our answer is found in Eph. vi. 17. "The sword of the Spirit, which is the word of God."[33]

The opening service was held on the first night, usually Thursday. Following the assembly of participants in the seats in front of the stand, the service began when a preacher started a spiritual song which was picked up by the congregation. There was usually no sermon in this service, nor in any night service; rather it was an alternation of ministerial exhortations and congregational singing. The alternation continued until mourners began to enter the pen, at which time the singing became a constant accompani-

---

[32] Timothy Flint, quoted in James Stuart, *Three Years in North America*, 2 vols., I, 175.
[33] In Mead, *Manna*, 39.

ment to the exhortations and invitations of the preachers. At some point the power of God came down, causing sinners to fall and more mourners to approach the altar, often with the aid of ministers and church members. The physical exercises, begun in the seating area, now centered in the pen. As soon as enough mourners had come forward, the ministers left the pulpit and moved into the pen themselves where they continued to exhort and invite and to counsel individual mourners. Good singers and praying persons also entered the pen, where they surrounded the fallen to give encouragement and comfort.

Some time between 10 P.M. and midnight—the time varied according to the success of the service—the crowd dispersed to tents, where the activities continued. Those who were still mourning continued to exercise, surrounded by sisters who sang and prayed in their behalf. Such activities could go on all night, with singing and shouting continuing as dawn broke.

About five the morning after the opening service, a trumpet signaled the time for family prayer in each tent. Following this, another trumpet was sounded, and everyone assembled around the pulpit for morning prayer. The content of this service varied, with some accounts reporting only prayer; others, public prayer, singing, and preaching. But by all accounts, the service was brief, ending for breakfast between half-past six and seven.

A third trumpet, sounded after breakfast, meant that it was time for morning service. A few of the participants moved into seats and started a spiritual song. They were joined by others until all were present, at which point the ministers moved to the stand. One would give out a prayer, and a sermon would then follow. Exhortations and invitations were sometimes issued in the morning services, but these usually failed to "strike fire," and there were soldom any mourners. More commonly the opening sermon was followed by testimonials from recent converts. Finally, at about eleven o'clock, the principal sermon was presented, often by a presiding elder or scheduled lay preacher, and this was the only occasion when a prepared address was deemed appropriate. Following the principal sermon, the congregation sang a closing song and then dispersed for lunch. The afternoon service was almost identical to that of the morning, except for the absence of a principal sermon.

During the break between afternoon and evening services, clergy gathered with lay people in private tents for services of singing, praying, and exhortation, accompanied by the usual physical exercises. Mrs. Trollope's description of private services is quite similar to her account of evening activities at the altar.

> We made the circuit of the tents, pausing where attention was particularly excited by sounds more vehement than ordinary. We contrived to look into many; all were strewed with straw, and the distorted figures we saw kneeling, sitting, and lying amongst it, joined to the woeful and convulsive cries, gave to each the air of a cell in Bedlam.[34]

Meanwhile other worshipers gathered at the altar for praying and singing. Such activities continued until dinner, after which, signaled again by a trumpet, evening services began.

Subsequent evening services differed little from those of the first night. Now and then a sermon followed the opening song, but this was optional and uncommon. At times the crowd remained assembled on the final night so that the meeting was continued until morning. But on all occasions it was at the evening services rather than those of the morning or afternoon that sinners were awakened and converted.

Two additional activities sometimes accompanied the camp-meeting. One was the "love feast," involving new converts, ministers, and church members. Coming near the close of the meeting, its purpose was the official induction of new people into the church. John Tevis, a Methodist preacher, described a Tennessee love feast in some detail.

> After sermon on Saturday, the *nature* and *design* of a Love-feast was explained, which seemed to excite a general wish to be present on the following morning; many attended—not less, it

---

[34] Trollope, *Domestic Manners*, I, 234.

is probable, than two hundred persons were admitted, one half of whom, perhaps, were not professors of religion. The meeting commenced with singing and praying; and the simple and eloquent manner with which many afterward testified the great things that God had done for them seemed entirely irresistible. The flame of love was soon kindled into rapturous joy in the hearts of the saints, while floods of tears involuntarily burst from the eyes of those who had been brought thither by idle curiosity, or had been induced to come with a desire to know the nature of our economy and to profit by our meeting. All appeared reverently to acknowledge that God was present in the assembly of his saints, and to feel that they were in the hallowed sanctuary of the Lord.[35]

Joining with the other saints in song and prayer and testifying to the change in their hearts, new converts were thus brought into the society of believers and made to feel a part of the group.

Special activities were also associated with the breaking up of the camp, when brethren bade each other an especially affectionate farewell. William Swayze, in a letter to the *Western Christian Monitor*, reported:

The meeting closed on Monday morning with exhortation; after which the people formed themselves into a large ring two deep, and marched around the camp ground, within the tents. They took leave of the preachers as they passed. Nothing of this nature could have been more affecting. Some came weeping and others shouting for joy; while some who had no religion wept and cried for bitterness of heart. The oldest preacher pronounced a blessing on the assembly; who then parted from each other in harmony and love.[36]

So affecting were such exercises that at a meeting held in Tennessee in 1820 a young convert stood on the seats and shouted to the congregation three times, "O Lord, must I go home and

[35] John Tevis, "Account of the Work of God in Holston District," *Methodist Magazine* 7 (1824), 351.
[36] *Western Christian Monitor* 1 (1816), 472–73.

leave these people and leave this place!" in a way that "seemed to penetrate every heart."[37]

The point of the camp-meeting activities was conversion, and every aspect of the meeting contributed to that end in one way or another. The organization of the camp-site was based upon conversion as one key discriminating attribute, for participants were kept apart on the basis of whether they had received grace. Exhortations were directed at winning souls to the way. Even the patterns of interaction among various groups of participants encouraged those outside the fold to enter in. But the camp-meeting consisted of more than effectively organized methods for bringing on conversions. It was a collective expression of the very idea of conversion, and the elements of the camp-meeting composed a structure parallel to the morphology outlined in the preacher autobiographies, except that the particular elements were expressed in group rather than individual terms. The collective expression of the morphology of conversion can be seen in everything from the camp site plan to the structure of preaching and singing to the kinds of interactions that took place among participants.

The camp-meeting site plan made for a highly structured situation which replicated the distinctions that existed in plain-folk society, as in sexual and racial segregation, and in the frontier sects, as in the physical distinctions made between leaders and lay people. This atmosphere was reinforced by the patterns of action in much of the ritual, particularly in its preconversion phases. The structures of exhortation, praying, and singing were identical, though manifested with varying degrees of subtlety. An exhortation, regardless of its specific content, elicited simultaneous audience response in the form of almost constant cries of "Amen!" or "Jesus!" or "Glory! Glory!" The minister took the initiative in issuing the exhortation, but the congregation signaled its admiration for his every word. A similar pattern existed in the sing-

---

[37] Letter dated Oct. 15, 1820, from Thomas L. Douglass to *Methodist Magazine* 4 (1821), 193.

Left: "The Morning of Life is gone—We are Journeying to that Land. Lorenzo Dow, Aged 39—(1816.)" *Right:* "From whence there is no return! Peggy Dow, Aged 35." From Dow, *History of Cosmopolite.* Photographed from a copy in the University of California, Berkeley, Library.

·A CAMP MEETING
OF the Cumberland Presbyterian Congregation, will commence on *Friday the 12th inst.* and continue four days, on the land of Parson Moore, on Cedar Creek.
Aug. 28.

Advertisement for a Cumberland Presbyterian camp-meeting, from the Selma, Ala., *Courier,* Aug. 28, 1828. From a copy of the newspaper deposited in the Alabama Department of Archives and History.

Left: Peter Cartwright, from *The Autobiography of Peter Cartwright* (New York, 1857). Photographed from a copy deposited in the University of California, Irvine, Library. *Right:* The Rev. James B. Finley. From *Methodist Magazine* 10 (1827). Photographed from a copy deposited in the University of California at Los Angeles Library.

Advertisement for a camp-meeting, which appeared in the Tuscaloosa, Ala., *Spirit of the Age*, Aug. 8, 1832. From a copy of the newspaper deposited in the Alabama Department of Archives and History.

CAMP MEETING.

A Camp-Meeting will be holden under the superintendence of the Rev. Dr. Kennon, to begin on Tuesday the fourth day of September, at the Buck-Spring Camp-Ground, four miles North of Tuscaloosa, on the Yellow creek road.

THE KNOXVILLE HARMONY

OF

MUSIC MADE EASY,

WHICH IS AN INTERESTING SELECTION OF

HYMNS AND PSALMS,

USUALLY SUNG IN CHURCHES:

SELECTED FROM THE BEST AUTHORS IN GENERAL USE.

ALSO,

A VARIETY OF ANTHEMS;

TO WHICH IS ADDED,

A NUMBER OF ORIGINAL TUNES;

BEING ENTIRELY NEW, AND WELL ADAPTED FOR THE USE OF SCHOOLS AND CHURCHES.

COMPOSED BY JOHN B. JACKSON.

TOGETHER WITH A COMPLETE INTRODUCTION TO THE PROPER GROUNDS OF VOCAL MUSIC,
AND RULES WELL EXPLAINED TO BEGINNERS.

D. & M. SHIELDS & CO., AND JOHN B. JACKSON, PROPRIETORS.

MADISONVILLE, TEN.

PRINTED BY A. W. ELDER.

1838.

164   Continued.   THE GOOD OLD WAY. L. M.

The queen of the world and the child, [of the skies

Lift up your heads, Immanuel's friends,   O halle,   halle - lujah,
And taste the pleasure Jesus sends,   O halle,   hale - lujah,

Let nothing cause you to delay, O halle, halle lu jah,   But hasten on the good old way, O halle, halle - lu - jah!

2 Our conflicts here, though great they be,
Shall not prevent our victory,
If we but watch, and strive, and pray,
Like soldiers in the good old way.

CHORUS.
And I'll sing hallelujah,
And glory to God on high;
And I'll sing hallelujah,
There's glory beaming from the sky.

3 O good old way, how sweet thou art!
May none of us from the depart,
But may our actions always say,
We're marching on the good old way,

Above: Title page to Jackson, *Knoxville Harmony* (Madisonville, Tenn., 1838). *Below:* "The Good Old Way," from Jackson, *Knoxville Harmony.* From the George Pullen Jackson Collection, Department of Special Collections, University of California at Los Angeles Library.

UNION HARMONY:

OR FAMILY MUSICIAN.

BEING

A CHOICE SELECTION OF TUNES;

SELECTED FROM THE WORKS OF THE MOST EMINENT AUTHORS,

ANCIENT AND MODERN.

TOGETHER WITH A LARGE NUMBER OF ORIGINAL TUNES,

COMPOSED AND HARMONIZED BY THE AUTHOR, TO WHICH IS PREFIXED A COMPREHENSIVE VIEW OF

THE RUDIMENTS OF MUSIC,

ABRIDGED AND ADAPTED TO THE CAPACITY OF THE YOUNG.

BY WILLIAM CALDWELL.

PRINTED BY F. A. PARHAM,

MARYVILLE, TENN.

1837.

Above: Title page to Caldwell, *Union Harmony* (Maryville, Tenn., 1837). *Below:* "St. Paul" from Caldwell, *Union Harmony.* From the George Pullen Jackson Collection, Department of Special Collections, University of California at Los Angeles Library.

ing. The minister initiated a song and then was joined by the congregation, and this pattern was further reflected in the verse-chorus structure of the camp-meeting spiritual songs. The verse, usually based on a regular church hymn, demanded some prior knowledge to be sung in a setting where either there were no books or it would have been too dark to use a book anyway. But the choruses were simple and redundant and were sung several times during a song; therefore everyone present could quickly learn the words and join in singing. Prayers, too, were patterned according to clergy-initiation–audience-response. The minister stood in the pulpit while members of the congregation knelt at their seats. As the minister prayed, the congregation responded with cries of "Amen!" or "Glory!" At other times, instead of shouting responses, members of the audience engaged in simultaneous individual prayers.

This patterning of activity set up a tension between the leader and his flock: there was a tendency toward group activity as the minister undertook no performance in which he was not joined by the congregation; however, the initiative remained with the clergyman, and the proper role of the congregation was that of response. It is significant that in accounts of discussions held prior to the meeting, invocation of the divine was carried on by the minister while lay people in no way tried to invoke the supernatural and confined their talk to sectarian concerns. The primacy of the preacher was further emphasized by his place on the stand, a man's height above both the brethren and the initiates.

As the conversion ritual itself began, one further separation was accomplished when mourners removed themselves from the church members and went into the pen. This was an acknowledgment, perhaps, that as convicted sinners they were not fit to mingle with the brothers and sisters in the congregation, a feeling which would have been reinforced by what the exhorters said of them. The exhortations were concerned with the depravity of man and his inability to overcome his own depravity without divine intervention. Designed to bring on conviction, exhortations attributed to all sinners a common uncleanness and moral impotence. Yet, when the mourners made their move into the pen, some drastic changes began to occur in the camp-meeting activities. First, the pattern of clergy-initiation–audience-response was broken. Congregational singing became a constant accompaniment to ministerial exhortations and invitations, leading to an equality in action, with each performance-group taking the initiative for its own activities. Second, in physical terms there was also an equality of position as the ministers stepped down from the raised stand to enter the pen where they continued their activities. The good singers and praying persons also entered the pen, thus canceling out their separation from the mourners while avoiding any further distinction between themselves and the clergy. Third, all accounts indicate that within the pen sexual segregations were either not pronounced or ceased to exist. Hence, no structural distinctions, except possibly racial ones, were in force in either physical setting or performance patterns.

During this period the power of God was operative in the gathering. Previously God's power was thought to have resided with the minister, as emphasized by his position above the throng. As he left his elevated platform and joined the mourners, the power of God was made manifest among the people in the behavior of the mourners—in convulsive physical exercises such as jerking and barking, or in the exhibited impotence of crying and trances. A stage was thus established which resembled the period of conversion as recounted in the preacher autobiographies. The main features of secular life had been condemned in the exhortations and symbolically rejected by convicted sinners who moved into the pen, where analogous structures in the meeting were purposefully negated. At the same time individual mourners manifested their own lack of control with the onset of exercises. Moreover, it was during the conversion period that women and children were allowed to serve as functionaries in the camp-meeting, either as convert-exhorters or as good singers and praying persons. Given the usual position of women and children in the religious organizations and in plain-folk society, their behavior here constituted a significant reversal of status, for those who were normally expected to take a subordinate role in life were here enabled to take control of a situation. Not only were the structures of the meeting —which replicated the social structure—purposefully negated, but for a time they were turned upside down. Then, as functionaries joined mourners in the pen, the "uncleanness" of the former sinners which had led to their earlier segregation was "washed away."[38]

The activities which took place in the pen during conversion were analogous to what the preachers had described in their autobiographies. Before it was possible to attain a new life, the old one had to be nullified. This was accomplished in the camp-meeting by the separation of the mourner from the sinful life as he left the old world and went into the pen. At that point the familiar social categories were also erased as social distinctions were dissolved. Thus, the "lost" feeling which accompanied the conversions of convicted individuals was replicated at the social level when familiar ways of relating to other people were temporarily suspended as statuses were reversed and other distinctions negated in the pen. It was only when the old world and the old ways of relating to others were no longer valid that a new world —ordered, it was believed, by God—could assume its rightful place. Camp-meeting leaders themselves recognized the importance of status and role reversals in the meeting. In the words of one Methodist writer:

> To see a *bold* and courageous *Kentuckian* (undaunted by the horrors of war) turn pale and tremble at the reproof of a weak woman, a little boy, or a poor African; to see him sink down in deep remorse, roll and toss, and gnash his teeth, till black in the face, entreat the prayers of those he came to devour; and through their fervent intercessions and kind instructions, obtain deliverance, and return in the possession of a meek and gentle spirit, which he set out to oppose;—who could say the change was not supernatural?[39]

---

[38] Van Gennep, *Rites of Passage.* My interpretation owes much to Victor W. Turner, *The Ritual Process.* To speak of having one's sins "washed away" was quite common in plain-folk religious expression.

[39] "Theophilus Armenius . . . Account," 305.

For the individual, the new life which he would receive from conversion was based on a certainty that he was beyond sin, an assurance of immortality, and a closeness to God. The result of a camp-meeting conversion was most clearly the incorporation of the new convert into the religious organization in the contest of the daytime services and in the love feast. In the morning and afternoon services the structure of the group was restored, and more concern was placed on the instruction of the saints than on conversion of sinners. The principal sermon was preached in the morning, whereas in the evening there was usually no sermon at all. A minister maintained the initiative throughout the day, except when a lay preacher was invited to speak, and even then the sermon was given by a person of high social status and did not differ in content from anything a regular clergyman might have said.

Church members derived the greatest amount of instruction from the sermons. Sermons and exhortations were often confused by outsiders and placed under the general rubric of "preaching," but in style and content, and in their places in the sequence of camp-meeting activities, the two forms differed greatly. The emotion-packed exhortations contrast sharply with the sermons, as described by the Swedish traveler Fredrika Bremer.

> At seven o'clock the morning sermon and worship commenced. I had observed that the preachers avoided exciting the people's feelings too much, and that they themselves appeared without emotion. This morning their discourse appeared to me feeble, and especially to be wanting in popular eloquence. They preached morality.[40]

The sermons were lengthy and concerned doctrinal or moral issues and were instructions in proper religious belief and behavior rather than invitations to sinners to give themselves up to the Lord. Furthermore, the preachers usually relied on prepared notes and based their sermons on specific Biblical texts, expounding in the

[40] Bremer, *Homes*, I, 312.

traditional fashion of text-context-application. Such instructional sermons were important in letting the new convert know what would be expected of him as a church member.

The new convert was also made a part of the group in the love feast, where testimonials were delivered. These were accounts of conversion which new church members delivered before clergy and older members. While the testimonies served in part as proof of the new convert's worthiness to become a member of the fellowship of believers and in part as an example for those who had not yet come to know salvation, the accounts of new converts were probably of greatest importance in their commonality with the experiences which all church members were thought to have had. Conversion was the basis of the frontier sects, and by giving his testimony, the newly minted saint was able to identify with that common foundation. His identification with the group was further enhanced in the love feast by the common singing of spiritual songs, an act in which the convert himself joined. Incorporation into the group was also emphasized in the closing service with its march around the campground, and the spirit of fellowship was what that service was mainly to convey. Indeed, there was no overt message which was preached at these closing services; rather there was the feeling of oneness expressed in the saints marching together and in the singing which usually accompanied their marches. Moreover, in the closing exercises, as in the conversion service itself, worldly statuses were again shunted aside in favor of common activity by a community of saints. In fact, there is even evidence that racial barriers were temporarily lifted in the "singing ecstasy" with which camp-meetings were brought to a close.[41]

So the convert, seeing his past life condemned beyond measure, went through a period during which any order he may have thought governed the world was systematically invalidated for him. As a result, he entered into a new world which was ordered on the basis of his relationship with the divine. The convert's place

[41] C. A. Johnson, *Frontier Camp Meeting*, 46.

in that world was maintained by his entrance into the community of saints that was the frontier sect. But what was the nature of that new world and of that community?

The frontier church-folk expressed their religious notions in the spiritual songs which were so important to camp-meeting activities. Like the camp-meetings in which they were sung, the spirituals were creations of the church-folk and in form and content comprised a type of song which was a response to the peculiar conditions imposed on the practice of religion by the frontier. The songs were quick tempoed and lively, and were distinguished from other forms of religious song—psalms and hymns—by the presence of a repeated and extremely simple refrain which appeared either by itself or attached to a verse:

> On Jordan's stormy banks I stand
> And cast a wishful eye
> To Canaan's fair and happy land
> Where my possessions lie.

Chorus:

> I am bound for the promised land,
> I'm bound for the promised land.
> O, who will come and go with me?
> I am bound for the promised land.[42]

In some parts of the country the songs were even called "choruses."[43]

Most of the verses were products of English hymnody and can be found without refrains in standard denominational hymnals from the nineteenth century. They were written by eighteenth-century English evangelicals including Samuel Stennett (who wrote the above example), John Cennick—whose "Jesus my all" was far and away the most popular source-hymn for spirituals—Charles Wesley, and Isaac Watts, the founder of modern English hymnody.

The choruses have no such pedigree. Their ancestry was not the

---

[42] John G. McCurry, *The Social Harp*, 114.
[43] Yoder, *Pennsylvania Spirituals*, 3.

literary tradition of the English hymn, but, as their greatest student George Pullen Jackson asserted, the "folky" hymns of eighteenth-century New England Baptists. The folk hymns were songs of praise which were simple and suited to group singing, and the spiritual choruses were "sung-to-pieces" versions of the New England Baptist hymns.[44] But even Jackson agrees that the responsibility for the manhandling of the songs rests with the camp-meeting Methodists on the Southern frontier. An early student of the form, B. St. James Fry, has described the process.

> At the commencement of the revival those familiar hymns, known to all our orthodox congregations, were used; but it was soon felt that they gave but imperfect expression to the ardent feelings of the worshippers. The deficiency here was principally supplied by the preachers. Hymns, or "spiritual songs," as they were more frequently called, to the cultivated ear rude and bold in expression, rugged in meter, and imperfect in rhyme, often improvised in the preaching stand, were at once accepted as more suited to their wants.[45]

The form was clearly useful to camp-meeting religion. Many people on the Southern frontier were illiterate, and the simple, repeated refrain made it possible for them to do away with hymn books but still join in the lively singing so suited to a revival. Additionally, many of the camp-meeting services were held at night when it would have been difficult for anyone to have read the words of a hymnal by the flickering torchlight that illuminated the evening sessions. It was also impractical to try to hold a book when, in pious joy, brother embraced brother. Finally, with the easily recognizable pattern of the spiritual songs, camp-meeting participants were able to retain many more songs in their memories than they might have otherwise.

Spiritual songs were disseminated among the people mainly through oral tradition in the context of the camp-meeting, but they were also written down, especially in the 1830s and '40s, by

---

[44] George Pullen Jackson, *Down East Spirituals and Others*, 3.
[45] "The Early Camp-Meeting Song Writers," *Methodist Quarterly Review* 41 (1859), 407.

the many "authors" of tune books. These authors conducted singing schools all over the frontier in order to supplement their
incomes from regular schoolteaching, preaching, or farming,
maintaining their schools by subscription and funds garnered
from the sale of tune books.[46] Both for convenience in teaching
and for success in sales, it behooved the authors to choose songs
which were known to be popular with potential students and
customers. Their books therefore were really compilations of what
one of them called the "unwritten music" of the church-folk, and
their activities those of folklorists preserving an oral tradition.[47]
That they succeeded, in their own terms, is shown by the fact that
one of the tune books, *The Southern Harmony*, first published in
1835, sold some 600,000 copies over twenty-five years, and it was
even sold in general stores, along with groceries and tobacco.[48]
As folksong collections which have survived to the present time,
the tune books are storehouses for the study of ante-bellum Southern religion.

Like their students, the tune-book compilers were not part of
the Southern elite. One of the earliest, Ananias Davisson (1780–
1857), was a Presbyterian elder from northwestern Virginia
whose first collection, the *Kentucky Harmony*, was published in
1816. His second, the *Supplement to the Kentucky Harmony*
(1825), may well have been the first tune book to include spiritual choruses, their presence explained by Davisson with the an-
nouncement that the book was to provide some good tunes for
his "methodist friends."[49] "Singin' Billy" Walker (1809–1875),

[46] Leonard Ellinwood, "Religious Music in America," in James Ward
Smith and A. Leland Jamison, eds., *Religious Perspectives in American Culture*,
302; George C. Eggleston, *The First of the Hoosiers*, 85; George Pullen Jackson, *White Spirituals in the Southern Uplands*, 237.

[47] William Caldwell, *Union Harmony: Or Family Musician*, 3.

[48] Mary Elizabeth Crutchfield, "The White Spiritual" (Thesis, Union Theological Seminary, 1946), 16.

[49] Ananias Davisson, *A Supplement to the Kentucky Harmony*, 3. Davisson's publication of spiritual songs may have been the first with music. The
many religious periodicals of the day often embellished their pages with
devotional poetry, and one of these periodicals printed, in 1803, a "Farewell
Hymn" which would later provide verses for a good many spiritual songs:
"Farewell my Friends, I must be gone—/I have no home nor stay with you;/

compiler of *The Southern Harmony*, was raised in Spartanburg, South Carolina. A Baptist, Walker put together several other books and traveled throughout the South setting up singing schools. It has been estimated that by the time of his death Walker's books had sold altogether about 750,000 copies.[50] B. F. White (1800–1879) was also born near Spartanburg, but lived in Georgia when he compiled his important *Sacred Harp*, a collection which has gone through many revisions and is still in print. A Missionary Baptist with but little formal education, White was a farmer and a dedicated singing teacher.[51]

Like Davisson, Walker, and White, most of the tune-book makers were from that area known as the Southern uplands, the center of plain-folk society and culture, and their biographies conform closely to the patterns of frontier life. Only one, James P. Carrell (1787–1854), was a slaveholder, but even he lived in the less fertile mountain area at the tip of Virginia. He was, in addition, an ordained Methodist preacher.[52]

The spiritual choruses, like the camp-meeting, were the creations of the frontier church-folk and were group religious statements which were sung by those who had been converted. Because of this, they add, as evidence, an important dimension to the study of camp-meeting religion. First, these songs were not the religious language of church leaders alone but were statements made by all the saints. As a result, they were unlikely to contain anything which was contrary to the beliefs held by most of the singers. While it is possible, from looking at the actions of camp-meeting

---

I'll take my staff and travel on/Till I a better world do view." This verse was later used for the spiritual song "Pilgrim's Farewell" which appeared in almost every collection. Other stanzas of the same hymn also appeared in other spirituals. In addition to the "Farewell Hymn," this same journal subsequently published "A New Spiritual Song," complete with both verse and chorus. Neither verse nor chorus, however, achieved any great popularity with Southern tune-book makers. For these examples see *The Western Missionary Magazine and Repository of Religious Intelligence* 1 (1803), 68, 108, respectively.

[50] G. P. Jackson, *White Spirituals*, 334.

[51] Ibid., 82–83.

[52] Gilbert Chase, *America's Music, from the Pilgrims to the Present*, 194.

MAP 3. Homes of songbook compilers, 1815–55.

saints, to get an idea of the kinds of things people thought to be effective in bringing on the power of the Lord and in bringing conversion, it is not possible to tell how the participants themselves interpreted what they were doing, and there is no reason why those who acted alike in the meeting should have given the same interpretation to their activities. Indeed, each participant could well have had a different idea about what actions had religious significance,[53] even though Methodist and Baptist preachers were at pains to ensure that such disagreements would not exist. The spiritual songs, however, may have been less subject to such differences in belief, for they were composed of those religious statements which *all* the participants were willing to make, and thus may well have represented the common denominator of plain-folk religious belief.

More than that, singing is a limited way of expressing ideas. The spiritual songs were highly redundant and quite brief, so that a single song could convey only a small amount of information. The effect was to force the song makers to rely on a set of stock phrases, devices, and poetic forms, limiting the songs to those matters about which the community was in substantial agreement. Further, the fact that most of the songs written down by the compilers were taken from oral tradition means that most of those which have survived to the present day consisted of motifs which were popular enough among religious plain-folk for people to want to remember the songs outside the camp-meeting context.[54] The spiritual choruses provided, then, a very good vehicle for plain-folk articulation of what the religious message of the frontier sects meant to them and of the nature of the new life given them by conversion.

[53] On this problem, see James W. Fernandez, "Symbolic Consensus in a Fang Reformation Cult," *American Anthropologist* 67 (1965), 902–29.
[54] Alan Lomax, *Folk Song Style and Culture*, 275.

IV

AND WE'LL ALL SING HALLELUJAH

The Religion of the Spiritual Choruses

CAMP-MEETING SPIRITUAL CHORUSES concisely summarized what religion meant to the frontier saints. Looked at by themselves, the words of the choruses seem very little different from most evangelical hymnody, and indeed they have been viewed as having little more expressive content than ejaculatory outbursts based on catch phrases; yet, in chorus composition the plain-folk were remarkably consistent, and very few individual choruses had themes which were incongruent with the main body of expression. More importantly, when viewed from the perspective of other frontier religious activities, the choruses can be seen to have formed a system of religious expression which was consistent with and which elaborated on both the camp-meeting and the experience of conversion.

One major theme ran through the choruses. Although the songs probably served several functions in camp-meetings—invitation, "pious ejaculation," prayer, or farewell—all were expressions of the assurance of salvation felt by the singers. There were great variations on the theme of assurance, but there was no variation in the feeling of certainty that each saint had of salvation. The choruses set forth, then, the various aspects of what salvation meant to most frontier saints.

That the brethren should have sung of their assurance is not surprising. All had been converted at some time prior to their singing of the spirituals, and each could rejoice in his destiny—

heaven. Moreover, the choruses were a vital part of camp-meeting activities, and the assurance they proclaimed was likely to have been useful in the conversion of new church members. The joy of the songs contrasted sharply with the hell-fire preaching of the exhorters, providing a dilemma for mourners in the period during which they were brought to the stand. When songs alternated with exhortations, the tension which had been present in performance patterns and in the structure of the setting was reinforced by the content of the two kinds of messages: just after the exhorter had reminded mourners of the nonregenerate sinner's doom, the congregation showed the would-be converts the joys of assurance awaiting anyone who had been saved. The structural tension of performance patterns was paralleled by a symbolic tension between heaven and hell. When the two forms of expression came to be performed simultaneously as meeting structures were broken down, the clarity of the opposition between the messages was also negated, forcing initiates to choose eternal life or eternal death. The resulting dilemma may have contributed in no small way to the frenetic quality of camp-meeting conversions; it certainly made the necessity to choose seem pressing.

While the saints were expressing their joy to those who had not known the fruits of conversion, they were also recounting what conversion had meant to them. The songs were probably not primarily didactic in character, for there were only a few which addressed the sinner directly. The saints sang of their assurance in the first person and in the songs were reliving their initial experience of the divine promise. Their songs were virtual descriptions of the conversion process, defining how that process should take place and what each saint could hope to achieve from it. Although the preachers in their autobiographies and preaching showed what the common denominator of conversion was to be for every frontier saint, the saints proclaimed in their songs what every frontier convert could readily give assent to—a consensus interpretation of conversion—and thus the songs articulated the common base of frontier religious belief.

Just as conversion was the core of the camp-meeting, so was it the foundation upon which the spiritual choruses were built.

When one received salvation, he entered into a new life that was diametrically opposed to the life from which he had come. Individuals described the old life as sinful and as a hateful thing, and they acknowledged the difference between old and new when they wrote of having given up former activities and former friends. This is what Dow meant when he said that his new life was like living as "a great speckled bird, among the birds of the forest, in the eyes of my friends."[1]

Camp-meeting activities also forced converts to break with the past before entering the new life. The whole thrust of the exhortations was to demonstrate the lack of virtue in the unconverted life and to reveal the sinner's doom. The conversion period itself was constructed in a way that symbolized the leaving of one life and entering of another as sinners entered the mourner's pen, as the structures of the meeting were broken down, and as individual mourners fell in an emotional frenzy.

This belief that conversion represented a departure from an old life is found in several motifs in the spiritual choruses which were illustrative of ways in which converts viewed their place in the world. The convert had gained a hope of heaven by his conversion, thereby receiving a very different way of looking at the world in which he waited for that hope to be realized. Mainly, the choruses reflected little feeling that any definite good, apart from conversion, could occur in worldly life. Instead, the saints sang of a world devoid of merit—indeed, hostile to them—but also of a world which would have to be endured for only a short time.

There were several variations on the central theme of world rejection, some more radical than others. The most common view was the most radical in the totality of its dismissal of the world and its commitment to the heavenly hope. This was the view expressed in such a chorus as

> To the land, to the land I am bound,
>   Where there's no more stormy clouds arising.[2]

---

[1] Dow, *Dealings*, 11.
[2] McCurry, *Social Harp*, 34–35.

The characterization of heaven as a place where the troubles of the world would cease was a summary of what the saints felt they had achieved by conversion. The storm image was a very old one in Christian language, and it has generally been used to describe a world in which the individual confronts little besides hostile forces which give him a constant lashing. Such a world is far from neutral, for it contains elements that frustrate people at every turn. The saints believed those frustrations to be the lot of everyone living in the world, and saw hope only in a distinct place. As they sang in another chorus:

> I want to go to glory.
> We have so many trials here below,
> They say there are none in glory.[3]

It was as if the trials, or stormy clouds, inhered in the world, so that the possibility of release was simply not to be found in the context of this life.

As a matter of fact, in several choruses the saints carried their world-rejection very near to its logical limits. In

> I'm a stranger,
> I'm a pilgrim,
> I can tarry but a night,[4]

the believers rejected the world absolutely and looked solely to the next. Describing themselves as "strangers," the saints acknowledged a sense of separation from the world, and when they claimed to be "tarrying" through what was undoubtedly a very dark night, they proclaimed the degree to which their conversion had led them to sever all ties with the life of the world. Again, believers made no commitments in this life, which was apparently devoid of religious significance, and salvation was to be realized only when they reached heaven.

The singers of this chorus also set forth a somewhat passive role for the saint. He was not to be engaged in any active preparation for heaven, but was merely to wait, as one chorus had it, for

[3] Ibid., 50.
[4] Ibid., 152.

the "sweet moments" to "roll on and let these poor pilgrims go home."[5] A sense of inevitability grew out of assurance, but it was a feeling that all but negated life, pointing instead toward death and the hereafter. A sermon preached at a camp-meeting took a similar point of view:

> Here is hope for the Christian; for the old pilgrim who is tempest-tossed and way-worn. Ah! this earth is not his home! Death is not an eternal sleep! He is journeying to a place that the Lord hath said, "I will give it you."[6]

Here, as in many spiritual choruses, the idea was that man did not make his way through the storm to arrive triumphant in heaven; rather, as he waited for the fulfillment of hope, the storms buffeted him. No real purpose was readily associated with the actual process of "going through," for all one's purposes were believed to lie elsewhere.

Other choruses were based on the same fatalism. When the saints sang,

> Carry me home, carry me home,
> When my life is o'er.
> Then carry me to my long sought home,
> Where pain is felt no more,[7]

they were again propounding a way of looking at the world which was quite thoroughgoing in its rejection. In the degree to which the plain-folk believers do appear to have given up on this life, they were going far beyond the evangelical religion out of which camp-meeting beliefs had developed. While their evangelical predecessors had sung of death, those earlier believers saw death as a fact rather than as an integral part of their hope. The length to which plain-folk went beyond them is shown in the difference between one of the hymns which provided verses for spiritual songs and the more traditional Methodist hymns upon which it was probably based. The spiritual verse was

---

[5] William Walker, *The Southern and Western Pocket Harmonist*, 165.
[6] In Mead, *Manna*, 302.
[7] B. F. White and E. J. King, *The Sacred Harp*, 387.

> I'm glad that I am born to die;
>> From grief and woe my soul shall fly,[8]

echoing the Wesleyan hymns "And am I born to die . . . ?" or "And am I only born to die . . . ?"[9] but taking a much different view of that necessary condition for the fulfillment of salvation. John Wesley, upon whose thought so much of camp-meeting religion was based, came close to such a view in those passages of his journal where he described dying friends as "waiting for the salvation of God,"[10] but many of the plain-folk said it even more forcefully. When the English travelers Reed and Matheson witnessed a deathbed scene in Virginia in the 1830s, they found the dying man looking only toward heaven:

> He spoke in the fulness of his heart; and the impression will, I trust, long remain with me. He told me of his early days, of his conversion, and of the many years he had been as a pilgrim and a stranger on earth. He had been married twice; he had lost his last wife seven years since; and his children had settled far from him. "Many expected," he said, "as I was living alone, that I should marry again. But, no, sir; at my time of life I think it not good. The husband careth for the things of the wife; but I wish now to care for the things of the Lord. My concern is, that I may do the will of the Lord, and look to my latter days with peace and pleasure. I would desire to die and be with Christ far better; but if he should say, Here, I have a little more for you to do on earth, then I would willingly stay and do it."[11]

Certain specific images in the choruses carried the same idea, especially those in which the saints sang of "passing over Jordan" on their way to heaven, as in

> And we'll pass over Jordan,
>> O, come and go with me;

---

[8] McCurry, *Social Harp*, 104.

[9] The derivation of the spiritual verse from the Wesleyan hymns was also noted in G. P. Jackson, *White Spirituals*, 240. Both hymns were written by Charles Wesley and may be found in *Hymns for the Use of the Methodist Episcopal Church*, 641 and 643, respectively.

[10] John Wesley, *The Journal of John Wesley*, 213.

[11] Reed and Matheson, *Visit to the American Churches*, I, 199–200.

> When we pass over Jordan,
> We'll praise th' eternal three,[12]

or, less explicitly, in

> I have but one more river to cross,
> And then I'll be at rest.[13]

Here the singers were proclaiming the one specific act that would get them to heaven: crossing the river that was death. When a dying Methodist woman was asked of her condition, she could only reply that she was, "Just on this side Jordan"—"My bodily affliction is great." Although she had led a good and faithful life, she knew its fulfillment could come only when she had crossed over, where pain would trouble her no more.[14]

The completeness with which they rejected the world was behind the plain-folk's thinking about most aspects of their religion. Just as the saints rejected worldly goals entirely, so were they wholeheartedly committed to the heavenly hope. They were, they said, strangers in this world, and they sang,

> Few days, few days,
> And I am going home.[15]

The saints sang of heaven as a "home" more than anything else. Though the image had been a part of Christian thinking since well before the Reformation and had been central to Puritan imagery in particular,[16] the symbol of heaven as a home was especially fitting to the frontier saints. If, after all, heaven were man's home, then earth could not be. Hopes were not to be ful-

---

12 Walker, *Southern and Western Pocket Harmonist*, 172.

13 White and King, *Sacred Harp*, 290.

14 "A Short Account of the Last Illness and Death of Susan Wyval," *Methodist Magazine* 1 (1818), 182. This interpretation of the "over Jordan" motif in the camp-meeting spirituals of Southern whites is supported in Theo Lehmann, *Negro Spirituals*, 309–10.

15 McCurry, *Social Harp*, 209.

16 The secular connotations of the word "home" were probably very great for a people as mobile as the Southern plain-folk, but the word came to them with a long history of usage in Protestant rhetoric about heaven. For the development and use of the term, see especially Haller, *Rise of Puritanism*, 149.

filled here below but had to wait for realization in another world. Often, when the saints sang of this home, they even added descriptions to emphasize its location, as when they sang of "my home high up in heaven." The description was not all that precise, but it did make clear that heaven was distinctly removed from this world. A Pennsylvania writer considered it essential that camp-meeting believers keep in mind that heaven

> is remote from this earth. Man has sought out many inventions, and among them, that this earth is to be the Christian's heaven. When Elisha's work was done, he mounted his fiery chariot, and went *up, away from the earth.* . . . Luke xxiv.51, 52.[17]

The Virginia saint, in the throes of death, told witnesses, "I am looking for something better:—earth will not do—this is not heaven!"[18] The plain-folk saw one major virtue of heaven in the idea that it definitely had nothing to do with the world.

The notion of heavenly distinctiveness was also expressed in a second major characterization of heaven, this one involving the use of the metaphor of a heavenly Canaan. This language was used in such choruses as

> I'm on my way to Canaan, to the new Jerusalem,[19]

and the very famous

> I am bound for the promised land,
> I'm bound for the promised land,
> O, who will come and go with me?
> I am bound for the promised land.[20]

Canaan language, like the symbolism of a heavenly home, is quite old and has important sectarian overtones, but world-rejection was also implied in the notion of a promised land that is to be reached at some future time. Derived from Old Testament imagery and having great currency among millennialists from the earliest days

---

[17] Mead, *Manna*, 353–54.
[18] Reed and Matheson, *Visit to the American Churches*, I, 200.
[19] McCurry, *Social Harp*, 204–05.
[20] John B. Jackson, *The Knoxville Harmony of Music Made Easy*, 48.

of Christian history,[21] Canaan language has long been associated with movements made up of people who view existing conditions as intolerable and hope for something different to be effected by divine intervention. The frontier saints were themselves looking for something different—conversion had given them an assurance that an alternative would be realized—but in explicitly tying the hope of a promised land with heaven, they made it clear that the alternative could not come to exist in this world. Relief from their situation was inextricably bound up in the hope of a world to come in another place.

Just as the heavenly hope was founded upon a rejection of the world, so was the frontier idea of God. In fact, the plain-folk composed very few choruses about God, and when they did, they usually created something similar to the following:

> And I'll sing hallelujah,
>> And glory be to God on high;
> And I'll sing hallelujah,
>> There's glory beaming from the sky.[22]

Theirs was a God in heaven, separated from the life of the world. The plain-folk never sang about any acts of God, just as they never spoke of His direct participation in the camp-meeting. They sang only of how man was to act toward God, and that was to be the act of praise which would take place in the future, when the saints had arrived in heaven.

Plain-folk belief in a God who was not so much of grace as of glory meant that His significance to the frontier saints did not lie in any function He might have performed, but rather in His mode of existence and in the relationship which the saints perceived themselves to have with such a being. The key word in the vocabulary of terms used to talk about God was indeed "glory," and the plain-folk used that word in three ways. First, they used it when they

---

[21] See R. H. Charles, *Eschatology*. For the role of these symbols in Christian millennial movements, see Norman Cohn, *The Pursuit of the Millennium*.

[22] William Walker, *The Southern Harmony, and Musical Companion*, 156. From THE SOUTHERN HARMONY SONGBOOK, copyright, by permission of HASTINGS HOUSE, PUBLISHERS.

talked about the kind of praise they would give to God. Second, they occasionally used it to describe the power which had converted them. Finally, they used it to talk about heaven and the mode of existence which they, too, would achieve when they had finally realized salvation. In their choruses about God the plain-folk were evoking, in other words, a state of being which corresponded to that which was most closely tied to their ultimate hope as saints, namely the state of glory which could be found only in heaven. Nevertheless, they were also acknowledging that in their conversions they had received a foretaste of what their glory would be like. The glory that was to be God's was, at the same time, a glory in which the saints themselves shared, and it was on this that their belief in God was founded. They were concerned with an ontological God rather than a functional one, for the mode of existence which they attributed to Him was symbolic of the ultimate hope they had for themselves.

In addition, such an ontological conception enabled the plain-folk to avoid the painful dilemma of Christian world-rejection. It would have been quite difficult for them to have reconciled a view of the world as devoid of good with a belief in God as the creator of all things, and, indeed, there are no spiritual choruses which propound such a notion of God. The saints resolved their potential dilemma by never connecting the will of God with the things of this world but by looking instead to another world, heaven, with which the divine will could be explicitly associated.[23] Plain-folk beliefs about God followed very closely their conception of the world.

Plain-folk world-rejection was quite thoroughgoing, at times approaching its logical conclusion in a death wish. Still, the saints were not really talking about a wish that would have been, after all, fairly simple to fulfill. The death of which they sang was a symbolic death indicative of the sharpness of that break with the old life which had to precede the new. The convert had begun his journey toward salvation with a powerful conviction of sin. To the extent that sinfulness had been an essential part of himself,

---

[23] S. G. F. Brandon, *The Judgment of the Dead*, 195.

as in fact it had been, that self had to be totally denied, and the person convicted at a camp-meeting could indeed be said to have been ritually dead. As earthly death was necessary to the assumption of eternal life in heaven, so was death of the sinful self a prior condition to the beginning of the new life of assurance.[24] The death talk of the choruses was less a wish for an event than a symbol of the kind of radical break with worldly life that conversion required.

This necessary break with the old life was the main point made by the world-rejection choruses, for such choruses indicated the great breadth and depth of that break. Though the plain-folk could specify certain activities that they considered sinful, the choruses showed that conversion was to mean something more than a marginal reform of one's behavior. The world that was rejected was universally bad. The "troubles" which confronted the saints were a part of the world's essential nature, and they saw no possibility that change in particular areas of life could make any difference to them or could provide relief from the causes of their pains. Characterizations of the world appearing in the choruses coupled with the saints' failure to see a place for the will of God in the world show very plainly how much the life of the saint was to differ from that of the sinner.

What, then, was the life of the saint to be like? Frontier conversion was not merely a negative phenomenon; indeed, negation occurred only as a first step. Converts felt they had received much that was positive from conversion, and in their songs of assurance the saints were most concerned to proclaim those positive aspects.

At the forefront was their assurance of an eternal life in heaven. The saints accounted the eternal life above all else, and their absolute certainty that the hope would be fulfilled lay behind each of the choruses. When they sang,

---

[24] The idea of "ritual death" is central to Mircea Eliade, *Rites and Symbols of Initiation*. The connection of this idea with the camp-meeting was briefly noted in Jerald C. Brauer, "Changing Perspectives on Religion in America," in *Reinterpretation in American Church History*, 26–27.

> I'll march to Canaan's land,
> I'll land on Canaan's shore,
> Where pleasures never end,
> And troubles come no more,[25]

they revealed no doubts about what the future held, and when each saint proclaimed,

> I feel like, I feel like I'm on my journey home,[26]

he told the world the source of his certainty. Conversion was not a matter of knowing, intellectually, that one had received a new life. Most commonly, frontier converts heard an inward voice or came to feel deeply and intensely that they had been saved, and such sensations were the source of each saint's assurance of a place in heaven.

Still, though by far the greatest number of spiritual choruses were about the assurance of heaven, there were few in which the singers got down to specifics in their descriptions of heaven. The saints sang of heaven mainly in terms of its distinctiveness from the world, calling it their home or a place "where pain is felt no more." The frontier heaven seems to have been more related to the believers' rejection of this world, and thus a negative end rather than a positive hope, but most likely the saints themselves viewed their heavenly destination in positive terms. So taken, plain-folk characterizations of heaven become most remarkable for their lack of specificity. It was not just that heaven differed from the world in certain important ways; rather, the plain-folk believed that there was nothing about heaven that was even remotely like the world. Their rejection of the world was total and general; hence, the other world to which the saint became committed also had to be totally and generally different.

Plain-folk ways of singing about heaven were influenced by the same considerations that affected their songs about God.

---

[25] Walker, *Southern Harmony*, 158. From THE SOUTHERN HARMONY SONGBOOK, copyright, by permission of HASTINGS HOUSE, PUBLISHERS.
[26] White and King, *Sacred Harp*, 154.

Again, plain-folk did not sing about acts of God in the world because, in the completeness of their world-rejection, they could find no aspect of the world with which to identify His will. Similarly, because their rejection of the world was total, neither were there aspects of the world which they could single out for special opprobrium. Their concept of heaven was structurally parallel to their concept of the earth in that just as they did not limit the generality of the world's evil by focusing on specific attributes, neither did they so limit the generality of their ultimate hope. The newness of the other world could only be shown as the saints had done, by proclaiming heaven's total distinctiveness from the sinful world which they endured.

Rejecting the world and hoping for a future post-mortem bliss did not leave the saint with nothing to show for his conversion while he remained in this life. For both traditional Protestant thought and that of the plain-folk, the conversion experience meant not only a deliverance from hell or an assurance of a place in heaven, but also a present change in the soul.[27] The convert received much to help him withstand the storms of life, and he sang in the spiritual choruses of what he had received.

If the saints rarely sang of God, they often proclaimed their faith in Jesus. Although they occasionally attributed a role to Jesus that was similar to that attributed to God, as in

> And Jesus stands a-waiting,
>   To welcome trav'lers home,[28]

it was more usual for them to look to Jesus to play a very active role in this world.

The church-folk thought of Jesus as, above all, the "Lord." As with all the saints' symbols, the term "Lord" has had a long history. Before it became a Christological title, the word was used in the Old Testament to refer to the God whose providence defended the nation of Israel. This Old Testament God was a functional

---

[27] Traditional ideas of conversion are discussed in Arthur Wilford Nagler, *Pietism and Methodism*, 125–26.

[28] Hauser, *Hesperian Harp*, 192–93.

deity, and the term came to be a title for Jesus that asserted His divinity, but on the basis of His present work in the world.[29] Such a functional conception was the basis as well for the plain-folk's use of "Lord," and they saw His present work as consisting in several activities.

The role of Jesus which the singers celebrated more than any other was that of the deity who converted and saved sinners:

> I never will forget the day
> When Jesus washed my sins away:
> And then my troubles will be over.[30]

This view of Jesus was very much a part of what the plain-folk believed conversion to be about, for if the old life of sin was to be totally denied, it was Jesus who made that denial possible.

The plain-folk's image of Jesus was inseparable from their approach to the question of the acquisition of grace, the thorniest of all religious issues discussed by Protestants during the first half of the nineteenth century. Although definitions of the nature of grace abounded among the various sects competing for plain-folk loyalty, probably the most salient was the Wesleyan doctrine which, institutionally, at least, claimed the widest adherence.[31] The phrase used by John Wesley as a summary of his version of the doctrine was that grace was "the entire work of God," meaning that grace was God's work both inclusively and exclusively. In the sense that grace was the inclusive work of God, its operation was the only activity directed from God to man; God therefore was always at work seeking out new souls in order to save them. Whatever other properties man may have ascribed to God were irrelevant beside this one great purpose to His work.

The second critical dimension to the phrase "the entire work of God" was that salvation could come by grace from God alone; hence the individual could do nothing more in his own behalf than to accept or reject God's offer of salvation. It followed that

---

[29] Oscar Cullman, *The Christology of the New Testament*, 207–08.

[30] McCurry, *Social Harp*, 85.

[31] The Wesleyan view even came to be adopted by non-Methodists who were purported Calvinists. See Boles, *Great Revival*, 138.

salvation came not from works but solely from faith.[32] "Faith" was itself a difficult concept to grasp, but one most commonly described in terms of assent. Saving faith meant, primarily, giving one's wholehearted assent to the divine offer of grace.

A good expression of the concept of grace in a spiritual chorus was:

> Hark! hark! 'Tis the voice of my Saviour and Lord;
> He calls unto me, "Poor Sinner, come!"[33]

As the saints recognized that it was Jesus who washed away sins, so did they recognize that the initiation of grace was an act of the Lord to which one convicted of sin was expected to respond. However, whereas Wesleyan doctrine made God the Giver of Grace, the saints assigned that role to Jesus. Doing so was consistent with camp-meeting practice in which Jesus, not God, had the central place; it was further consistent with the ontological conception of God propounded in the choruses. Because God was wholly other than the world, Jesus took on the functional role of initiator of grace.

The distinction between ontology and function was an important part of plain-folk thinking about the divine. The two divinities were conceived as distinct and coequal, and Jesus was never spoken of as the "Son of God." Furthermore, there was never any controversy over the uniting of the two natures of God and man in Christ.[34] Because of their definition of Jesus, the saints could easily sing,

> How charming is Jesus!
> He is my Redeemer, my Lord and my God.[35]

---

[32] Robert E. Chiles, *Theological Transition in American Methodism, 1790–1935*, 29–31. Philip Wesley Ott, "The Mind of Early American Methodism, 1800–1844" (diss., Univ. of Pennsylvania, 1968), 119–20.

[33] Walker, *Southern and Western Pocket Harmonist*, 164.

[34] Such a concern was absent from even the writings of academic Methodist theologians. See Ott, "Mind," 89–90.

[35] Hauser, *Hesperian Harp*, 319. The word "charming" deserves a comment. Don Yoder points out that "The medieval hymns of the Savior, and the

To the plain-folk, Jesus was wholly divine, but His divinity rested squarely on His activities as Redeemer and Lord.

The plain-folk also articulated the distinction they perceived between God and Jesus when they directed a different kind of praise toward each. Praise to God was identified with the glory of the heavenly estate and was almost always described as a future activity rather than one which could occur in the world. Praise to Jesus occasionally took the same form, but it was more likely to take place in the here and now:

> Hallelujah! hallelujah! hallelujah!
> I love the Lord:
> This note above all others raise,
> My Jesus has done all things well.[36]

Believers could direct praise to Jesus in this life, and it was based on what the saints thought He had done.

One very important thing the saint received from conversion, then, was the knowledge that a being wholly divine had taken an interest in his mortal soul. It was not just that there was a general offer of grace which one could accept or reject, but rather that the Lord had made the offer to each individual as an individual. As it was put in the chorus, "He calls to *me*, 'Poor Sinner, come!'" The saints were concerned, again, with the *present* work of Jesus as it related to every individual.

Not surprisingly, the plain-folk showed little interest in the historical Jesus outside of one event, the crucifixion. The death of Jesus on the cross was not important as an event that had happened eighteen-hundred-odd years earlier, but as an act which was as relevant to people of the nineteenth century as it had been to

---

pietistic *Jesuslieder*, praised the 'loveliness,' accented the compassion, exalted the Lordship of Christ. Bernard's 'Jesus the very thought of Thee with sweetness fills the breast' is not far in spirit from the Pennsylvania spiritual *O vee leeblich*." (Yoder, *Pennsylvania Spirituals*, 45n). "*O vee leeblich*" was a Pennsylvania German translation of "How charming . . ." except that Jesus was a "friend" to the Pennsylvania singer, not a "God."

[36] Walker, *Southern Harmony*, 326. From THE SOUTHERN HARMONY SONGBOOK, copyright, by permission of HASTINGS HOUSE, PUBLISHERS.

people of the first. Moreover, it was an event by which the Lord could relate to each individual. One preacher remembered:

> When I was on my knees crying to God for a full Deliverance I heard a voice inwardly say, "I have sealed the pardon of thy sins with my blood." I felt the truth of it in my heart, and in a moment prayer was turned into praises,[37]

and the plain-folk put the same feeling into song:

> I will believe, I do believe,
> That Jesus died for me,
> Remember all thy dying groans
> And then remember me.[38]

If the convert received nothing else, he could at least take some measure of satisfaction in the feeling that the Lord had taken an interest in *his* fate as an individual and that there was a divine commitment to see the saint in glory.

Such knowledge did, in fact, give the believer a new perspective from which to consider the world. Though the church-folk saw no evidence of God's will around them, they could nevertheless sing of the Lord that

> Jesus reigns he reigns, victorious
> Throughout heaven and earth most glorious
> Jesus reigns![39]

They propounded a similar idea, but with a millennial bent, when they sang,

> Glory, honour, and salvation;
> Christ, the Lord, is come to reign.[40]

---

[37] In Sweet, IV, *Methodists*, 126.

[38] White and King, *Sacred Harp*, 368. Variant: "Remember, *Lord*, thy dying groans...," Walker, *Southern Harmony*, 324. One should also note the parallel between the significance assigned to Jesus' death and rebirth and the symbolism of death and rebirth in the plain-folk's conversion and salvation.

[39] Caldwell, *Union Harmony*, 91. Variant: "*over* heaven and earth...," Walker, *Southern Harmony*, 146.

[40] Caldwell, *Union Harmony*, 148. Several choruses besides this one drew

Such choruses seem at once to have been contrary to plain-folk world-rejection, but they must be viewed in the light of the camp-meeting and conversion, and more especially in light of the place assigned to Jesus in both events.

The Lord entered into plain-folk conversion and into camp-meetings during the period when converts had, on the one hand, rejected their old life but, on the other, had not yet entered into the new. According to plain-folk beliefs, the individual could not move himself from the one state to the other; that transition was accomplished by the intervention of the Lord.

Camp-meeting choruses celebrating Jesus' reign display a strikingly similar structure. There was no greater opposition in plain-folk religious thought than that between heaven and the world. Yet, just as divine intervention was able to bridge the gap between sinner and saint, so was the lordship of Jesus thought to reconcile the seemingly irreconcilable opposition of earth to heaven, not so much as a result of His having combined both divine and human natures, a matter of little or no concern to frontier saints, but rather as a product of His ability to *act* in both spheres, and particularly of His ability to carry human beings from one sphere to the other.

It may seem strange that the same saint who could sing

> This world's a wilderness below
> This world is not my home,[41]

---

on millennial imagery. I tend to think, as this chapter should make clear, that these choruses do not represent a millennial hope so much as another perspective on assurance and on the place of the Lord in the world, particularly in the camp-meeting. Nevertheless, John B. Boles has shown that there *were* strong millennial hopes accompanying the Great Revival that spawned camp-meetings, and choruses about those hopes—few in number by the 1840s—could have been survivals from an earlier day. See Boles, *Great Revival*, 100–10. That great latter-day Son of Thunder, Peter Cartwright, appears to have dismissed millennialists as hopeless fanatics whose chief heresy, aside from visionary practices, was their belief that paradise could come to exist on earth rather than only in heaven. See *Autobiography*, 51–52, 273–75.

[41] White and King, *Sacred Harp*, 310.

could also exclaim,

> I'm happy, I'm happy,
> May the Lord continue with me,[42]

but both choruses are consistent with plain-folk beliefs about what constituted Jesus' lordship. Although the saints rejected the world in and of itself, they also recognized that the operation of grace took place in the context of this life, and, moreover, that the relationship established with the Lord at conversion was to be an ongoing one from which the saint could derive continuing satisfaction.

In recognizing that Jesus could make one "happy" and that an aspect of His lordship was His sovereignty over heaven and earth, the saint was in no sense accepting the world as given. Deriving satisfaction from what Jesus did in the world, the frontier believer nonetheless acknowledged that the main purpose of the Lord's activity was to assure each individual a place in *another* world, heaven. Assurance could give one a sense of worth and a great amount of joy *in* the world, but that did not mean that one became happy *with* the world. Indeed, the feeling of having risen above the world through one's relationship with the Lord was a major part of what it meant to be saved.

The plain-folk understood that assurance of an eternal life in heaven could come only after an intensely personal experience of the power of the Lord, so that much of their singing about salvation was in the first person singular. Camp-meeting religion has been described as highly individualistic in its concern for the individual soul, and because of the centrality of religious experience, one could not expect otherwise. Very often, however, the church-folk sang of salvation in more collective terms, as when they rejoiced,

> Hallelujah! hallelujah!
> We are on our journey home.[43]

---

[42] McCurry, *Social Harp*, 62.

[43] Walker, *Southern Harmony*, 327. From THE SOUTHERN HARMONY SONGBOOK, copyright, by permission of HASTINGS HOUSE, PUBLISHERS.

Such a group consciousness appeared in a large proportion of the choruses[44] and encompassed several ideas about what conversion meant.

The notion of a heavenly recongregation—a belief that groups of the saved which existed temporarily on earth would reassemble for an eternal existence in heaven—was almost as important to the saints as was their belief that heaven meant an end to earthly troubles. Recongregation choruses such as

> Oh, may we meet in heaven;
> In heaven alone, no sorrow is found,
> And there's no parting there,[45]

or

> Farewell, brethren; farewell, sisters,
> Till we all shall meet again [above, at home][46]

were probably sung at the close of a camp-meeting to accompany the breaking of camp and the parting of the fellowship of believers until some future meeting, but each believer looked forward to a heavenly meeting where brethren and sisters should never be required to part again.

The Canaan imagery which the saints used in reference to heaven also had strong sectarian overtones. The idea of a heavenly Canaan has traditionally stemmed not simply from a feeling that heaven was different from the world but, more, from a feeling that the hope of heaven grew out of a special promise made by the Lord to His people. There was, in other words, a sense of unity, of peoplehood, involved in the metaphor of a heavenly Canaan as well as a hope of a new world. At one level, this sense of unity grew out of a feeling of exclusivity which was part of how the saints saw their religious organization. Since only those who had been converted by the divine were eligible for church

---

[44] About one-third of the choruses emphasized the importance of the group. In addition, nouns and pronouns denoting the group are about the same in number as those denoting the individual.

[45] McCurry, *Social Harp*, 60.

[46] Walker, *Southern and Western Pocket Harmonist*, 151.

membership, the frontier sects were not organizations to which everyone could belong, but were organizations in which membership was seen as something every individual had achieved by responding to the Lord's offer of grace. The Canaan terms were a recognition that, on the frontier, the saints alone were the recipients of the divine promise of salvation.

More than this, the recongregation choruses and the Canaan imagery showed the believer that, by his salvation, he had become part of an eternal community, stretching backward to include God's first "chosen people" and forward to eternity. This idea was conveyed especially well when the saints sang,

> Oh what a happy time, when the Christians all get home,
> And we'll shout and praise the Lamb in Glory.[47]

Such a view of their relationship vis-à-vis some eternal community gave each saint a new way of looking at himself, and it also gave him a new outlook on the group of which he was a member in this world. During the march around the campground which often closed a meeting, the parting brethren might sing, for instance,

> We're marching through Immanuel's ground,
> And soon shall hear the trumpet sound,
> And then all shall with Jesus reign,
> And never, never part again.[48]

The saints felt that during the camp-meeting they had succeeded in bringing the converting power of the Lord into the world where, while they met, the operation of His grace had been made manifest. Where the brethren were, in other words, was where the Lord worked in the world. It was as though their gathering had taken a portion of the earth and caused it to be in the world, but

---

[47] White and King, *Sacred Harp*, 377. Variant: ". . . when the Christians all *shall meet to* shout. . . ," Walker, *Southern and Western Pocket Harmonist*, 166.

[48] White and King, *Sacred Harp*, 294–95. Variant: "We soon shall hear the *welcome* trumpet sound, / O, *there* we shall with Jesus *dwell.* . . ," Walker, *Southern Harmony*, 198.

no longer of the world. The sect, as a community of the saved, had closer ties with the eternal community in heaven than with the society of sinners around it.

Plain-folk believed that they derived much from their membership in the community. For one thing, they felt that in being part of the group their chances of withstanding the storms of life were greatly improved. The saints viewed the sect as an active organization which, though their hopes remained with the world to come, was a source of strength for each member. In thus viewing themselves as part of the church when they sang

> O come, and join our pilgrim band,
>   Our toils and triumphs share;
> We soon shall reach the promised land,
>   And rest forever there,[49]

or

> We'll stem the storm, it won't be long,
>   The heav'nly port is nigh,
> We'll stem the storm, it won't be long,
>   We'll anchor by and by,[50]

the saints found reason to look for more than just escape from the world. The storm could perhaps be weathered, and though life may have posed some threat to believers, it also could be viewed as a challenge which the church member was enabled to accept with an assurance of victory.

Their need to withstand the storms came from the frontier belief about what was required of the saint after his initial reception of grace. Among the more Calvinistic Presbyterians and Baptists, it was officially held that "the saints will finally persevere through grace to glory,"[51] meaning that with the giving of grace at the time of conversion, the Lord had given the convert knowledge that there was a place in heaven for him which could not be

[49] Hauser, *Hesperian Harp*, 172.
[50] White and King, *Sacred Harp*, 378.
[51] Doctrinal statement of a Kentucky Baptist church, reprinted in Sweet, I, *Baptists*, 180.

lost. For the Methodists, however, perseverance was conditional upon the maintenance of one's saving faith. According to official doctrine:

> After we have received the Holy Ghost, we may depart from grace given, and fall into sin, and by the grace of God, rise again, and amend our lives. And therefore they are condemned who say they can no more sin as long as they live here . . . .[52]

This originally Methodist idea of conditional perseverance came to dominate all camp-meeting religion, and the possibility of backsliding, or falling away from grace, was impressed on every convert. Although constant vigilance was one way of avoiding that possibility, the saints also felt that membership in the community of the saved could be of great help in guaranteeing the completion of the journey to heaven.

According to B. St. James Fry, a writer contemporary with the spiritual singers, "the most frequent and vivid conception of the Christian life in the minds of these hardy pioneers, was that of an active, unceasing warfare."[53] The brethren might well exhort each other to

> Never get tired a-serving of the Lord;
> Come along, and shout along, ye heaven-borne soldiers;
> Come along, and shout along, and pray by the way.[54]

Or they might express the hope of heavenly reward by urging their brethren:

> Crying amen, shout on till the warfare is over, hallelujah![55]

The martial imagery was considerably more activist than were many of the motifs associated with world-rejection, perhaps because group membership gave the saint a strength which, alone, he did not possess. Each of the camp-meeting choruses about the warfare contained an exhortation to other saints to participate in

---

[52] *Doctrines*, 10.
[53] Fry, "Early Camp-Meeting Song Writers," 408.
[54] McCurry, *Social Harp*, 184.
[55] Walker, *Southern Harmony*, 314. From THE SOUTHERN HARMONY SONGBOOK, copyright, by permission of HASTINGS HOUSE, PUBLISHERS.

the common enterprise of praying and shouting their way into heaven.

Such activities were the essence of what it meant to serve the Lord. Plain-folk ideas of stewardship were at once quite limited and all-inclusive, as were their ideas of heaven: they did not want to be tied down to specifics. Believing grace to be "the entire work of the Lord," following Wesley, the saints saw their duty as consisting solely in responding to the Lord's call and, having once responded, making sure they did not backslide and fall away from grace. The need for militant symbols was stimulated by the recognition that backsliding was a real possibility, and indeed keeping "heaven in view" in a world so profoundly separate from it and from God must have been a major feat. But they knew that success meant more than a future seat in paradise, for strength of faith was, as one anonymous Methodist put it, "a means of glorifying God" while one remained in this life.[56]

The martial choruses implied the importance of all the soldiers to the perseverance of each saint. Other choruses were more explicit, as when the singers proclaimed,

> 'Tis religion we believe,
> O, glory, hallelujah!
> Soon it will land our souls up yonder;
> Glory, hallelujah! [57]

and

> When we get to heaven we will shout aloud and sing,
> Shout glory, halle, hallelujah!
> Religion is a fortune,
> And heaven is a home.[58]

"Religion" was assigned a mediating role similar to that of the Lord, but where Jesus had made the heavenly hope seem real to each saint through conversion and the "washing away" of sin,

---

[56] "Means of Confirming a Weak Faith," *Christian Advocate* 10 (1832), 240. See also Hill, *Southern Churches in Crisis*, 80.

[57] Walker, *Southern and Western Pocket Harmonist*, 112–13.

[58] McCurry, *Social Harp*, 42.

religion provided the ongoing support necessary to enable each saint to persevere to glory.

The plain-folk sang often of the community of saints, and it is not surprising that they should have done so. Most church members had received their initial supply of grace through conversion at a camp-meeting—that is, through participation in the activities of the community—and each could "shake the manna tree" for a fresh supply whenever the saints gathered together.[59] Moreover, conversion was always consummated by the integration of each new saint into the existing community. The discipline to which all members of frontier sects were subjected and the support and watchfulness of one's fellow Christians were excellent safeguards against falling into sin. Ultimately, there were also the ties between the sect of which the frontier saint was a member and the eternal church in heaven which each member was sure to join. The individual was not alone in a world which was a sea of hostile forces, but he could see himself as a part of something much larger that transcended the particularities of his own time and place.

The group-centered choruses which proclaimed a recongregation of the saints in heaven expressed an idea that has often been a part of the beliefs of sects in which members are converted in a clear and definable way—that is, the idea that the church visible, in the world, is identifiable with the church invisible, in heaven. Since all of those who are members of the church on earth have had to undergo conversion and hence are definitely assured of a place in heaven, it stands to reason that the community of saints in heaven will be identical to, and is thus an extension of, the community of saints that exists in the world.[60] The frontier saints sang of their belief in the purity of their own churches when they sang their spiritual songs, and the belief came through in other forms of religious discourse as well. Pious church-folk on their deathbeds often would welcome death and their impending arrival in heaven as a chance to "be in the society above," and to rejoin their "pious acquaintances who have departed this life and gone to their reward

[59] Yoder, *Pennsylvania Spirituals*, 456–57.
[60] Morgan, *Visible Saints*, 1–4.

on high."[61] Others drew on their belief in the purity of the frontier church when, like Jacob Young, they looked back on earlier days with such words as, "Many of my most valuable acquaintances had gone from the Church below to the Church above."[62] In so conceiving their religious communities, frontier believers were acknowledging that becoming a part of the eternal fellowship of saints was a major aspect of what their conversions had meant.

The dominant concern of frontier religion was with the individual soul, its conversion and ultimate salvation. Still, the saints gave a major place to the sect as the agency whereby one could persevere on the heavenly journey, and they saw membership in an eternal, never-dying community of saints as an ultimate end to that journey. The individual, it is true, was and had to be the object of converting power, but the sense of belonging to God's eternal church was an inseparable part of every individual's salvation.

In general, the themes of the spiritual choruses were consistent with the main outlines of conversion as recounted in the preacher autobiographies and as that experience took place in the camp-meeting. The choruses emphasized rejection of the world as a step necessary to entering upon the life of the saint, the role of the divine in effecting conversion, and the end of salvation as life in a heaven that was diametrically opposed to this world. Where the songs parted from the accounts in the preacher autobiographies, as in assigning to Jesus the power of conversion and in the emphasis on membership in the community of saints as a goal in salvation, as well as in the generality with which the world was rejected, the songs seem to have followed very closely the way in which camp-meeting participants likely perceived what went on in the meeting. The preachers could talk, for example, about the power of God falling on a meeting, but participants directed their anguished cries to Jesus. Their leaders could come out of conversion with a feeling of sinlessness and of an individual relationship with the Lord, but their followers might look mainly for a hope of

---

[61] S—— W——, "A Short Account of the Life and Death of Mrs. Mary Baily," *Western Christian Monitor* 1 (1816), 284.

[62] Young, *Autobiography*, 337.

heaven and find great comfort in being members of that fellow-ship which the frontier sects offered. In the spiritual choruses, in other words, the saints were articulating not what religion was supposed to mean to them, but what it *did* mean to them—their understanding of what they were taught—and though the form was taken from their teachers, the content was specifically relevant to their needs.[63]

Conversion gave every convert a new way of looking at the world—the old life was utterly and completely rejected upon con-version and replaced by a positive response to the Lord's offer of grace. The saint's response therefore gave him an outlook on life in which the hope of heaven came to replace the transitory and trivial goals of this world and in which each could perceive his place in a larger community from which he could draw strength and sustenance. Such a new outlook was particularly suited to the people of the Southern frontier.

---

[63] On this point one should add a brief comment about the verses to which spiritual choruses were attached. In general, as noted in ch. III, the verses were drawn from "official" church hymnody, while the choruses were the compo-sitions of the plain-folk themselves. The two elements seem to have been virtually independent, as there were no clear rules for verse-chorus combina-tion. A single hymn might be combined with many different choruses, on several themes, just as the plain-folk could attach a given chorus to any one of several verses. As at least one writer has pointed out, there was no necessary connection between the subject of the hymn and the content of the chorus (see Louis F. Benson, *The English Hymn*, 293). Still, there was one important relationship between the verses and choruses, beyond the fact that the choruses made it possible for everyone who desired to join in camp-meeting singing. The evangelicals who wrote the hymns were much more concerned than the frontier saints for the Christian life. There is none of frontier religion's radical world-rejection to be found in the hymns, and though the basic images of a heavenly bliss and a saving Lord are common to both verses and choruses, the evangelical hymn writers gave their treatment of those images a decidedly this-worldly orientation. Just as the choruses made the hymns practically singable, they also made the hymns intellectually singable. The choruses served to re-orient the verse to the plain-folk's own way of looking at religion by em-phasizing those elements of the hymn which were compatible with frontier belief and by providing a summary, which everyone joined in singing, of what the hymn was all about. (On the relationship of "choruses" to "verses," of nonexplicit to explicit elements in poetry, see Dell Hymes, "Some North Pacific Coast Poems: A Problem in Anthropological Philology," *American Anthropologist* 67 [1965], 316–41.)

V

WE'LL STEM THE STORM

Plain-Folk Religion and Frontier Life

THE PLAIN-FOLK EXPRESSED their religious beliefs in the traditional language of Protestant Christianity, but the old symbols took on new meaning in the context of life on the Southern frontier. Enormous problems confronted the frontier farmer and his family, but the vital conversionist camp-meeting religion which the plain-folk created for themselves helped to ease those problems by giving people hope where there had been little before.

The plain-folk were at the margin of ante-bellum Southern society. Not really poor, they were nevertheless outside the major political and economic processes of the South. However much they wanted to break into the Southern system, there were few openings, and most people who were not born in the planter elite never entered it. There were, to be sure, avenues of mobility allowing some plain-folk to rise to the top of Southern society, but those who did were not numerous. Their success served mainly to keep amibition alive in the great mass of small farmers destined for lives of disappointment.

Frontier religion offered the plain-folk an alternative to what was essentially a closed system. Institutionally, the sects were organizations in which members could achieve some measure of control over their lives and could also attain some degree of status. The Baptist churches were organized into fairly autonomous congregations which had broad jurisdiction over the everyday lives of individual members. Not only did congregations watch over each Baptist's social behavior, discouraging such vices as drinking, gambling, and fighting, but congregational disciplines also covered members' dealings in the economic sphere. Where secular authority was lacking, or where its exercise was closed to the plain-folk, the sect provided alternative ways for members to exercise authority, giving them some role in making the crucial decisions that affected their lives. Further, since every member of the congregation had a hand in administering the congregational discipline, channels of authority were open to all Baptists. Much the same can be said of the Methodist discipline, at least in the sense of its provisions for the comprehensive regulation of members' social and economic lives, although the hierarchical organization of the church limited the number of plain-folk who directly participated in administration.

The sects also offered possibilities for personal advancement. Most Baptist churches were led by farmer-preachers who worked their fields for a living, but were enabled, because of their gifts, to lead local groups. While preachers received no pay for their church labors, a poor but gifted young Baptist could at least attain some place of respect within the local community. Methodism offered even greater opportunities for personal advancement. A gifted male Methodist could rise far beyond the level of the local congregation to have jurisdiction, as a presiding elder or even as a bishop, over a group of churches covering a vast geographic area.

Such were the opportunities for individual plain-folk who were both gifted and male. But every believer could feel he had achieved something, for membership itself was not possible without effort. Conversion was required of all who would be church members, and even though grace was believed to come only from the Lord, frontier religious thought also recognized that the divine offer was made to everyone. The saint was not distinctive in his having been chosen for salvation, but still, in having given himself up to the Lord when he accepted a grace freely and universally offered, the frontier church member had set himself apart from most people. In addition, the believer retained his distinctiveness by maintaining his faith, for the way of the backslider was also open to all. Plain-folk thought, as articulated in the revival spirituals, included both free grace and conditional perseverance, each of which placed a requirement of assent and continued effort on the believer's shoulders.

The main feature of the distinctiveness which the saints had come to possess was, according to their songs, the assurance of salvation. Conversion had given each church member a hope of heaven, and it had further placed each convert into a personal relationship with the divine. The brethren described that latter relationship, for example, when they sang of how the Lord Himself had saved them or how in Jesus they had found a personal Lord. For the individual this meant that what Jesus had done when He died on the cross and in His role of Saviour had been done for each and every believer. The saints were fond of saying that "Jesus died for me, even me." Such knowledge was a source for personal esteem, as each saint realized that conversion had come as a result of his own significance in the eyes of the divine.

The brethren expressed the same feeling in group terms when they sang about Canaan; the frontier saints, like the ancient Israelites, felt themselves to be the recipients of a direct promise from the Lord. Just as God had vouchsafed to those ancient people a home in the promised land so long as they remained faithful, so had He promised the Christian believers an eternal place in the heavenly Canaan as a reward for their perseverance. The divine promise, which the frontier sectarians had freely accepted, set them apart from and above their benighted peers, for their conversions had given them a unique place in His plan for the whole world. However much they might wander through the wilderness of this life, they were sustained by a higher purpose embodied in the promise of an eternal life of bliss in the world to come.

The saints' sense of distinctiveness was enhanced by their rejection of the life of this world. While they exalted what conversion had made them and the hope it had given them, they denigrated what they had been and the world from which they had come. Their hope of heaven was clearly intended as an alternative to the goals of this world, and its superiority was explicitly asserted when they defined their aim in terms that were more negations of this world than pie-in-the-sky symbols of the next. The plain-folk hope of heaven was not merely an otherworldly, escapist device; rather, it was a setting of a goal which differed significantly from those of the secular Southern world.

World-rejection was at the very heart of frontier conversion experiences. The one who came under conviction saw his life in the world as a hateful thing and the goals he pursued as objectionable goals. Even though, when the convert got down to specifics, he would invariably mention only the most obvious vices such as drinking or gambling, it was his whole life and the whole world he had turned his back on.

The spiritual choruses displayed the depth and breadth of world-rejection. When the saints sang of the world in their choruses, they sang of it in terms of its general lack of merit. The world was, by contrast with heaven, a place of constant travail, marked by endless troubles and a sea of "stormy clouds." The specific vices which they often identified with the life of the world, when seen in the light of attitudes expressed in the choruses, took on symbolic as well as practical value. The saints, by classifying such common vices as taboo, were enabled to make their rejection of the world a concrete act as well as an intellectual belief. It would have done them little good to have forbidden activities in which they could not possibly have participated, but in focusing upon the most popular frontier recreations they were able to demonstrate the force of their beliefs in their daily lives. What they were in fact rejecting was of far greater breadth and far less specificity than frontier fun because, as they proclaimed in their songs, salvation had meant a release from the whole world and not merely the sort of marginal reform which would have been effected by moderation in all things. They emphasized the thoroughness of their rejection of the world, moreover, in their failure to sing about any connection between God and the events around them, and the mediating Saviour was similarly at work in the world only as an agent for leading converts to the next. Thus, while personal conversion accounts and church discipline aimed at stamping out the most obvious frontier evils, such taboos were merely the practical fruits of the view expressed in the choruses that evil pervaded the whole world.

One, of course, would not expect the saints to go into great detail in singing about the sources and nature of evil, just as in their invitation choruses one could not expect to find much about the sinner's doom and the torments of hell. Such topics were for exhorters to take up, and the saints themselves were much more interested in talking about what religion had given them as converts. Further, in the context of their services the choruses fitted into a symbolic pattern offsetting the exhorter's fearsome threats with a message of hope and assurance. Therefore songs of evil would have been out of place. What is more remarkable is that the saints were as vague about what conversion had given them as they were about what that experience had removed them from. The individual convert had exchanged the general troubles of the world for the hope of a trouble-free eternal life in heaven, but what heaven was to be like was never specified. Nor, perhaps, could it have been. The saint did not seek a release from certain aspects of the life of the world as much as he sought a replacement for his entire world. Since the believer was most concerned with heaven's distinctiveness, this was the feature upon which he concentrated in his singing. To have been more specific about heavenly attributes would have been to place limits on the wholeness of what the heavenly alternative had to offer.

Similarly, the saints were quite vague about the process by means of which they had achieved their new outlook. Compared to the conversions of many other peoples, the religious experiences of the plain-folk were not especially vivid. While other Christians have reported seeing the Lord face-to-face or journeying to the portals of heaven and the gates of hell, the plain-folk were likely, at most, to hear a voice or, more commonly, to feel from within the assurance of salvation. Although the physical and psychological symptoms of conversion were certainly overpowering and the experiences they signaled were unforgettable, plain-folk conversions were not marked by the kinds of vivid spiritual events that are often found in such experiences. There was, in other words, in plain-folk conversion accounts a lack of specificity in descriptions of both the agency and the ends of the conversion experience itself.

This very vagueness in their experiences of conversion and in their talking about both the world they had rejected and the hope they had gained is a clue to how the plain-folk perceived their place in the Southern order. The frontier folk were outside of an economic system based on plantation agriculture, and the steady expansion of that plantation system kept all but the luckiest and most able of them in their marginal position. Yet, the plain-folk's reaction to their continued marginality was never clear-cut. On the one hand, they seem to have borne some resentment toward the planters as a class. When opportunities arose, there were several movements among plain-folk to wrest control away from the elite, and the farmers often spoke bitterly of the plantation owners and their aristocratic ways. Still, when they had to choose, the plain-folk almost invariably came down on the side of the South and the Southern way of life, meeting even the supreme test in the Civil War. The frontier farmers were as dedicated to the South as the planters were, so that if they often felt bitter about their own position in Southern society it was more because they had not entered fully into its economic activities than because of any dreams of a more democratic system. They had ambitions, but their ambitions were well within limits posited by the Southern order.

Moreover, the amount of resentment they focused on the planters was not very great, partly because the plain-folk were connected with the elite by ties of ambition and, in many cases, family. The numerous movements among some plain-folk to break planter power were usually unsuccessful, largely because of the lack of widespread support among the rest of the farmers. These people wanted to become planters themselves, and indeed enough of their number did move up to indicate to those who had not that the possibility of making it was still there.

There was, then, a certain lack of clarity in the plain-folk's perception of their place in the Southern world. Just as the saint could not specify the precise nature of the troubles of the world or the nature of the release which conversion had given him, the frontier farmer could not define the cause of his own frustrations. He knew he could not realize his ambitions, but he was not capable of pinpointing what had caused his failure—nor was he ever likely to identify the cause, for it lay within the very plantation system which he had wholeheartedly accepted and which he so longed to enter. Thus, since he could identify no concrete villains in his assessment of his plight, the frontier farmer saw himself as living in a world which was generally unfavorable to him, and he saw his life in that world as the object of hostile forces which he could neither understand nor control.

The solution offered by the religious alternative accepted those hostile forces as simply a part of this world, indeed, as this world's essential nature. Hence, the sheer distinctiveness of the heavenly alternative was what appealed to the converts. There was no question of pointing to a heaven in which specific difficulties were ameliorated—as when, for example, black Americans have sung of a heaven where discrimination would be absent or, again, when millennial movements have posited a nativistic future or have taken a revolutionary turn. Because the plain-folk could spot no specific cause of their troubles and because their own ambitions prevented them from looking for areas of change in this life, the heavenly hope had to be wholly other than what this world had to offer.

The drastic alternative of heaven provided an answer to a major problem which the plain-folk faced in their ante-bellum Southern society. Predicated on a thorough rejection of the life of the world, it was a solution which demanded much of the frontier folk who embraced it; they had to forgo many of the pleasures to which their unconverted neighbors could escape in order to make a difficult life more tolerable. But the alternative offered in reward a new perspective on life in which the believer no longer had to see himself as a failure in a particular social system but as one who had achieved the ultimate success. His lack of material success could thus be accounted for as an understandable product of living in a hostile world, and he could now reorient his life in terms of the more important goal of a life in heaven—a goal which he could feel sure to achieve.

The frontier folk faced pressures originating from within as well as from outside their communities, and these pressures too were addressed by camp-meeting religion. The worst problems were drunkenness and brawling, two not unrelated forms of frontier recreation. The sects were able to overcome those difficulties within the limits of their memberships through preaching and teaching and through a rigid enforcement of their disciplines. Whatever the symbolic import of the taboos on frontier vice, prevention of those activities by the sects also had the salutary effect of keeping the faithful away from liquor and out of trouble.

The camp-meeting, too, was likely to have had a valuable practical function in providing a ready substitute for the more spectacular forms of recreation. The frontier world was a difficult one, and no doubt drinking, gambling, and brawling all provided a temporary escape for the frontier folk. All were intense, exciting experiences enabling each participant momentarily to "lose himself" and thus to ignore the ongoing drudgery and frustration that were the small farmer's lot. The camp-meeting made for a similarly intense and exciting experience for its participants. The meetings allowed the plain-folk to leave their farms for a few days of fellowship, and the emotional frenzy which was reached by many participants at the meetings was almost certainly a release from the kinds of tensions that could build up during a year of life on the frontier.

Yet the frontier vices and the need for a release which they, like the camp-meeting, provided were but symptoms of a deeper problem facing the small farmer on the frontier. The problem grew out of two major sources, one being the Southern social system in which the individual farmer could make but little headway toward realizing his ambitions and the other lying within the plain-folk communities. People on the Southern frontier were faced with a need to cooperate in a variety of ways with their neighbors. Group labor was essential to the maintenance of their farms, to the preparation of land for farming, and to the harvesting of crops. In addition, neighborly cooperation was a kind of frontier social security system, so that when any one family in a neighborhood faced disaster, the whole community would contribute to softening the blow. Their migratory way of life further forced the plain-folk to depend upon others because no one could travel very far in search of new land without joining others in a band or counting on the hospitality of settlers along his route. For those who settled, a homestead could not be easily established without the aid of those already in the new area.

Such a source of security was indispensable to plain-folk, but there is much to suggest that cooperation did not come naturally to them. The fact that supposedly cooperative ventures were organized competitively was one indication of this; another indication was the brawling which was so much a part of community affairs. One reason for the difficulties the plain-folk had in reconciling themselves to the neighborly system was that the kind of person the farmers appeared to have admired most was not the kind of person who could fit easily into a cooperative mode of action. The frontier heroes, at least as described in folktales and legends, were all rugged individualists, men little given to politeness or to a willingness to subordinate individual desires to common good. To be a *real man*, in the eyes of plain-folk, was to be a self-sufficient and unrestrained individual.

Frontier brawling, while it may have been an outlet for tensions, was also an attempt on the part of participants to be like the heroes of frontier yarns. Faced with a failure to achieve his ambitions and with the recognition that he could not even survive on his own, the frontier farmer might well have used fighting to reassert his manhood. The gap between the man the farmer felt he should be and the man he knew he actually was could be bridged by a kind of hedonistic individualism which was mainly asserted through braggadocio and violence. By such a chip-on-the-shoulder aggressiveness, the frontiersman attempted to emulate his heroes, and hence to make himself more like the man he felt he ought to be. The solution, however, was less than satisfactory in what it did for the quality of life on the Southern frontier.

Camp-meeting religion provided a better solution to one aspect of the problem by positing alternative goals, and thus alternative ambitions which could be satisfied within the framework of Southern society. Religion provided an answer as well to the gap between the frontier credo of individualism and the need for neighborly cooperation. It did so by giving the individual a new basis for self-identification; this fresh identity was established in the camp-meeting and was explained by the spiritual choruses. Camp-meeting conversion was a three-stage process leading ultimately to membership in a frontier sect. The conversion services began with participants arranged in a way that conformed to the manner in which Southern society was itself arranged, especially in terms of the distinctiveness of sex and religious roles and in racial segregation. Then, at the height of conversion activities, this structuring of the setting was completely broken down as mourners, saints, and preachers entered the pen together. More, the original structure was actually turned upside down, for not only did everyone enter the pen, but people who were ordinarily assigned a subordinate place in Southern life, the women and children, actually assumed leadership of the activities in their roles as counselors and, in the case of new converts, as exhorters. The period of structural negation corresponded in a religious sense with the period of personal conversion during which one lay convicted of sin, but the negation may have served a social function as well. To the extent that one draws much of his orientation to himself and to other people from the kind of social structure in which he participates, the negation of structure in the conversion period must have had the effect of invalidating the secular images of self and society which most plain-folk had. Both men and women were undoubtedly affected by the reversal which found a normally subordinated sex assertive to the point of assuming practical leadership. Moreover, the whole thrust of the frontier credo—which urged every person to attempt to get the better of every other person—was effectively blunted by the equalizing ceremony of the glory pen where brother embraced brother in a common joy. This spirit of community was emphasized even more strongly in the closing exercises culminating in a march around the encampment with all the saints joining hands and singing.[1]

The new orientation which the saint received from his participation in camp-meetings was outlined in the spiritual choruses. In the same way that sect membership was an ostensible end of camp-meeting conversion, so was membership in the community of saints believed to be valuable for its own sake. The idea that every sect member was also a part of the community of saints which existed eternally in heaven was back of several motifs in the choruses, including those of recongregation and those in which the singers proclaimed their place in a pilgrim band and their destiny to join the army of the Lord. In addition, the belief in the value of the community was very much a part of the songs which drew upon the image of a heavenly Canaan, whereby the saints tied their own ultimate hope of heaven to their feeling of being a chosen people. The identification of the sect with the heavenly hope occurred in one way or another in a substantial number of the spiritual songs.

There was more than one way of looking at what conversion meant. The predominant view, expressed in the choruses, focused on the salvation of the individual soul, as each saint rejoiced in song at his own assurance of a place in heaven. Yet, there was an undercurrent of group feeling as well which was proclaimed when the brethren sang of an eternal community of the saved into which each frontier convert had entered.

In this, camp-meeting religion helped to overcome the gap between the plain-folk image of what one ought to be and what conditions made one by altering the image. It was not merely that sectarian membership gave the frontiersman a group to join, although that may have been part of it, but rather that religion forced the convert to orient himself to a new view of what his proper place in life ought to be. No longer did he see himself in

[1] For a full treatment of this idea from a cross-cultural perspective, see Turner, *The Ritual Process*.

terms of the rugged, self-sufficient individualism of the secular world. Following conversion, the saint recognized that he was part of and could draw his strength from an eternal community founded by the divine and identified with mankind's ultimate hope. The convert's values were no longer founded on the hedonistic individualism of the frontier, but upon a desire to maintain the place in the community of saints which each member had achieved by his conversion. Belief meant a complete redefinition of self in corporate rather than autonomous terms.

George Santayana wrote:

> every living and healthy religion has a marked idiosyncrasy; its power consists in its special and surprising message and in the bias which that revelation gives to life. The vistas it opens and the mysteries it propounds are another world to live in; and another world to live in—whether we expect ever to pass wholly over into it or not—is what we mean by having a religion.[2]

The plain-folk received "another world to live in" as a result of conversion. At one level, that other world was a heaven where their troubles would end forever; yet they also received "another world to live in" while they remained in this life. The saints described their new world in the language of evangelical Protestantism, but what they described was distinctly relevant to the place and time in which they lived.

The people of the frontier were certainly in dire need of such a new world. While it is true that people in most societies feel a lack of correspondence between their view of how things ought to be and the way things actually turn out to be, that gap was particularly troublesome to the plain-folk. Much as they desired to advance socially and economically, they were frustrated in achieving their goals by the very system in which they hoped to succeed. Believing in liberty and self-sufficiency, they were forced into a relationship of mutual dependence with their neighbors if they were even to survive.

---

[2] George Santayana, *Reason in Religion*, quoted in Clifford Geertz, "Religion as a Cultural System," in *The Interpretation of Cultures*, 87.

Camp-meeting religion helped to bridge the gap between secular ideals and the reality of Southern life by offering a new set of ideals which plain-folk could, with effort, attain. On the one hand, there was indeed a connection between secular ideals and those of religion which probably made the message of the camp-meeting more easily acceptable, for religious ideals responded to secular needs. Religion offered, especially, an opportunity for each individual to feel that he had control over his own life since a basic tenet of frontier belief was that one was saved by making a conscious, affirmative answer to the offer of grace. Although the convert came under the discipline of a larger group in ways that governed a good part of everyday life, no one could become subject to that discipline or remain under its control without first having given consent to do so. More than that, in choosing to heed the call of the Lord, each convert took a step which would assure his ultimate destiny for a life in heaven. Through religion, then, the individual received a degree of self-esteem and self-determination that was equally important to a secular person, but which the latter could not hope to attain.

Despite the basic connection of the religious message to secular values in the appeal each made to the individual will, however, the goals which the individual was fitted for in each realm were diametrically opposed. Whereas the secular individual sought to express himself in a competitive environment by achieving a position of economic or, failing that, physical superiority over others, the saint, in choosing religion, agreed to subordinate himself to a community that acted in accordance with what was believed to be the divine economy. A saint thought that his life, after conversion, was totally unlike what it had been before, and in terms of his goals and ideals that was the case.

The opposition between secular and religious ideals probably accounts for much of the frenetic quality of camp-meeting conversions. In choosing to "turn" to the Lord, the frontier convert was making a definite commitment to turn his back on long familiar goals and to adopt not simply new modes of behavior but, in fact, a new way of life and a new way of looking at the world. Discarding what one had been, in favor of becoming a very different person, could not but have required a tremendous amount of mental and emotional effort at the moment a commitment was made, and the opposition between one's old "sinful" self and the self one became upon conversion meant that the convert's break with the past had to be complete; his belief in the new world, wholehearted.

Life on the Southern frontier was not easy for the plain-folk, and their religion was addressed to its hardships. Created on the frontier, camp-meeting religion consisted of forms and expressions which had developed as immediate answers to the practical problems posed by sparse population and general infidelity. The final product was not based upon book learning and theological speculation but upon practices and beliefs that successfully jibed with the thinking and feelings of the frontier settlers. The other world which camp-meeting religion propounded was the other world the plain-folk of the frontier needed.

BIBLIOGRAPHY

PRIMARY SOURCES

Tune Books

Caldwell, William. *Union Harmony: Or Family Musician.* Maryville, Tenn.: F. A. Parham, 1837.

Carden, Allen D. *The Missouri Harmony.* Cincinnati: Morgan, 1836.

————. *United States Harmony.* Nashville: J. S. Simpson, 1829.

————, Samuel J. Rogers, F. Moore, and J. Green. *Western Harmony.* Nashville: The compilers, 1824.

Cayce, Elder C. H. *The Good Old Songs: A Choice Collection of the Good Old Hymns and Tunes as They Were Sung by Our Fathers and Mothers.* 22nd ed., Thornton, Ark.: Cayce, 1960.

Clayton, David S., and James P. Carrell. *The Virginia Harmony.* 2nd ed., Winchester, Va.: Robinson and Hollis, 1836.

Davisson, Ananias. *A Supplement to the Kentucky Harmony.* 3rd ed., Harrisonburg, Va.: The author, 1825.

Jackson, John B. *The Knoxville Harmony of Music Made Easy.* Madisonville, Tenn.: D. & M. Shields, and John B. Jackson, 1838.

Hauser, William. *Hesperian Harp.* [Philadelphia, 1848.]

Leonard, Silas W., and A. D. Fillmore. *The Christian Psalmist.* 10th ed., Louisville: n.p., 1851.

McCurry, John G. *The Social Harp.* 1855; rpt. Philadelphia: S. C. Collins, 1868.

Metcalf, Samuel L. *The Kentucky Harmonist.* 4th ed., Cincinnati: Morgan, Lodge, and Fisher, 1826.

Moore, William. *Columbian Harmony.* Cincinnati: Morgan, Lodge, and Fisher, 1825.

Swan, M. L. *The New Harp of Columbia*. Nashville: W. T. Berry, 1867.

Walker, William. *The Southern and Western Pocket Harmonist, Intended as an Appendix to the Southern Harmony*. Philadelphia: Thomas Cowperthwaite, 1846.

————. *The Southern Harmony, and Musical Companion*. "New Edition, Thoroughly Revised and Much Enlarged." Philadelphia: E. W. Miller, 1854; rpt., New York: Hastings House, 1939.

White, B. F., and E. J. King. *The Sacred Harp*. "New and Much Improved and Enlarged Edition." Philadelphia: S. C. Collins, 1860.

Source Documents

The biographies, autobiographies, periodicals, and travelers' accounts listed here but not cited in the notes were necessary to the delineation of the structures of conversion and/or camp-meetings.

Allen, W. F., Charles P. Ware, and Lucy McKim Garrison. *Slave Songs of the United States*. 1867; rpt., New York: Peter Smith, 1951.

Asbury, Francis. *Journal of Rev. Francis Asbury, Bishop of the Methodist Episcopal Church*. 3 vols. New York: Lane and Scott, 1852.

Beauchamp, William. "Revivals of Religion Among the Methodists," *Western Christian Monitor* 1 (1816), 373–74.

Birkbeck, Morris. *Notes on a Journey in America from the Coast of Virginia to the Territory of Illinois*. Philadelphia: Caleb Richardson, 1817.

Boom, Aaron M., ed. "Texas in the 1850's, as Viewed by a Recent Arrival," *Southwestern Historical Quarterly* 70 (1966), 281–88.

Bremer, Fredrika. *The Homes of the New World: Impressions of America*, trans. Mary Howitt. 2 vols. New York: Harper, 1854.

Broadbury, John. *Travels in the Interior of America in the Years 1809, 1810, and 1811 (Early Western Travels, 1748–1846*, ed. Reuben G. Thwaites. 32 vols., vol. V). New York: AMS Press, 1966.

Cartwright, Peter. *Autobiography of Peter Cartwright, the Backwoods Preacher*, ed. W. P. Strickland. New York: Carlton and Porter, 1857.

Cuming, Fortescue. *Sketches of a Tour to the Western Country through the States of Ohio and Kentucky (Early Western Travels*, vol. IV). New York: AMS Press, 1966.

Davidson, Robert. *History of the Presbyterian Church in the State of Kentucky: With a Preliminary Sketch of the Churches in the Valley of Virginia*. New York: Carter, 1847.

Dow, Lorenzo. *The Dealings of God, Man, and the Devil; as Exemplified in the Life, Experience, and Travels of Lorenzo Dow, in a Period of Over Half a Century.* 4th ed., Norwich, Conn.: William Faulkner, 1833.

————. *History of Cosmopolite; or the Four Volumes of Lorenzo Dow's Journal Concentrated in One, Containing His Experience and Travels, from Childhood to Near His Fiftieth Year.* 5th ed., Wheeling, Va.: Joshua Martin, 1848.

Drake, Daniel, M.D. *Pioneer Life in Kentucky, 1785–1800,* ed. Emmet Field Horine, M.D. New York: Henry Schuman, 1948.

Eggleston, Edward. *The Circuit Rider: A Tale of the Heroic Age.* Lexington: Univ. of Kentucky Press, 1970.

Eggleston, George C. *The First of the Hoosiers: Reminiscences of Edward Eggleston.* Philadelphia: Drexel Biddle, 1903.

Evens, Estwick. *Pedestrious Tours, 1818* (*Early Western Travels*, vol. VIII). New York: AMS Press, 1966.

"Evidences of a Weak Faith," *The Christian Advocate* 10 (1832), 189–92.

Faux, William. *Memorable Days in America: Being a Journal, 1823* (*Early Western Travels*, vols. XI, XII). New York: AMS Press, 1966.

Finch, I. *Travels in the United States of America and Canada.* London: Longmans, Rees, Orme, Brown, Green, and Longman, 1833.

Finley, James B. *Autobiography of Rev. James B. Finley; or, Pioneer Life in the West,* ed. W. P. Strickland. Cincinnati: Methodist Book Concern, 1853.

Finney, Charles G. *Revivals of Religion.* Abridged ed., Chicago: Moody Press, 1962.

Flint, James. *Letters from America, 1818–1820* (*Early Western Travels*, vol. IX). New York: AMS Press, 1966.

Flint, Timothy. *Recollections of the Last Ten Years, Passed in Occasional Residences and Journeyings in the Valley of the Mississippi, from Pittsburgh and the Missouri to the Gulf of Mexico, and from Florida to the Spanish Frontier.* New York: Knopf, 1932.

Fry, B. St. James. "The Early Camp-Meeting Song Writers," *Methodist Quarterly Review* 41 (1859), 401–13.

Gallaher, James. *The Western Sketch Book.* Boston: Crocker and Brewster, 1850.

Gorham, B. W. *Camp Meeting Manual, a Practical Book for the Camp Ground.* Boston: H. V. Degen, 1854.

Hall, James. *Legends of the West*. Philadelphia: Harrison Hall, 1832.

————. *Letters from the West: Containing Sketches of Scenery, Manners, and Customs; and Anecdotes Connected with the First Settlements of the Western Sections of the United States*. 1828; rpt. Gainesville, Fla.: Scholars' Facsimiles and Reprints, 1967.

Hamilton, Capt. Thomas. *Men and Manners in America*. Philadelphia: Carey, Lea and Blanchard, 1833.

James, Edwin, comp. *An Account of an Expedition from Pittsburgh to the Rocky Mountains, Performed in the Years 1819, 1820 (Early Western Travels*, vol. XIV). New York: AMS Press, 1966.

Lee, Jesse. *A Short History of the Methodists in the United States of America Beginning in 1766, and Continued till 1809*. Baltimore: Magill and Clime, 1810.

McClure, David. *The Diary of David McClure, Doctor of Divinity, 1748–1820*. New York: Knickerbocker Press, 1899.

Marryat, Frederick B. *A Diary in America with Remarks on Its Institutions*. 6 vols. London: Longman, Orme, Brown, Green, and Longman, 1839.

Martineau, Harriet. *Retrospect of Western Travel*. 3 vols. London: Saunders and Otley, 1838.

Maximilian, Prince of Wied. *Travels in the Interior of North America (Early Western Travels*, vol. XXIV). New York: AMS Press, 1966.

Mead, A. P. *Manna in the Wilderness; or the Grove and Its Altar, Offerings, and Thrilling Incidents*. Philadelphia: Perkinpine and Higgins, 1859.

"Means of Confirming a Weak Faith," *The Christian Advocate* 10 (1832), 237–41.

Methodist Episcopal Church. *The Doctrines and Disciplines of the Methodist Episcopal Church*. 14th ed., New York: John Wilson and Daniel Hitt, for the Methodist Connection, 1808.

————. *Hymns for the Use of the Methodist Episcopal Church*. Rev. ed., New York: Carlton and Porter, 1849.

————. *Minutes of the Annual Conferences of the Methodist Episcopal Church for the Years 1773–1839*. 2 vols. New York: Methodist Episcopal Church, 1840.

Methodist Magazine and Quarterly Review

Michaux, François André. *Travels West of the Allegheny Mountains, 1802 (Early Western Travels*, vol. III). New York: AMS Press, 1966.

Milburn, William H. *Ten Years of Preacher Life: Chapters from an Autobiography.* New York: Derby and Jackson, 1859.

Olmsted, Frederick Law. *A Journey in the Back Country.* 1860; rpt., New York: Burt Franklin, 1970.

Raumer, Frederick von. *America and the American People,* trans. William W. Turner. New York: J. and H. G. Langley, 1846.

Reed, Andrew, and James Matheson. *A Narrative of the Visit to the American Churches, by the Deputation from the Congregational Union of England and Wales.* 2 vols. New York: Harper, 1835.

Ricker, Joseph. *Personal Recollections: A Contribution to Baptist History and Biography.* Augusta, Me.: Burleigh and Flynt, 1894.

"Rural Life in Ante-Bellum Alabama," ed. Walter F. Peterson. *Alabama Review* 19 (1966), 137–46.

S—— W——. "A Short Account of the Life and Death of Mrs. Mary Baily," *Western Christian Monitor* 1 (1816), 283–84.

Semple, Robert B. *A History of the Rise and Progress of the Baptists in Virginia,* rev. and extended by Reverend G. W. Beale. Richmond: Pitt and Dickinson, 1894.

"A Short Account of the Last Illness and Death of Susan Wyval," *Methodist Magazine* 1 (1818), 181–83.

Strickland, William P. *The Life of Jacob Gruber.* New York: Carlton and Porter, 1860.

Stuart, James. *Three Years in North America.* 2 vols. New York: Harper, 1833.

Tevis, John. "Account of the Work of God in Holston District," *Methodist Magazine* 7 (1824), 351–52.

"Theophilus Armenius." "Account of the Rise and Progress of the Work of God in the Western Country," *Methodist Magazine* 2 (1819), 184–87, 221–24, et passim.

Tocqueville, Alexis de. *Democracy in America,* trans. Henry Reeve. 2 vols. New York: Co-operative Publication Society, 1900.

Trollope, Frances. *Domestic Manners of the Americans.* 2 vols. London: Whittaker, Treacher, 1832.

Welby, Adland. *A Visit to North America and the English Settlements in Illinois (Early Western Travels,* vol. XII). New York: AMS Press, 1966.

Weld, Isaac. *Travels Through the States of North America.* 2 vols. 1807; rpt. New York: Johnson, 1968.

Wentworth, Erastus. "Methodists and Music," *Methodist Quarterly Review* 17 (1865), 359–77.

Wesley, John. *The Journal of John Wesley,* ed. Nehemiah Curnock. Abdgd. ed., New York: Capricorn, 1963.

Western Christian Monitor (Chillicothe, Ohio, 1816).

Western Missionary Magazine and Repository of Religious Intelligence (Washington, Pa., 1803–1805).

Woods, John. *Two Years' Residence in the Settlement on the English Prairie, in the Illinois Country (Early Western Travels,* vol. X). New York: AMS Press, 1966.

Wright, John F. *Sketches of the Life and Labors of James Quinn, Who Was Nearly Half a Century a Minister of the Gospel in the Methodist Episcopal Church.* Cincinnati: The Methodist Book Concern, 1851.

Young, Jacob. *Autobiography of a Pioneer; or, the Nativity, Experience, Travels, and Ministerial Labors of Rev. Jacob Young, with Incidents, Observations, and Reflections.* Cincinnati: L. Swormstedt and A. Poe, 1858.

Zuber, William Physick. *My Eighty Years in Texas,* ed. Janis Boyle Mayfield. Austin: Univ. of Texas Press, 1971.

Printed Source Collections

Botkin, B. A., ed. *A Treasury of Southern Folklore: Stories, Ballads, Traditions, and Folkways of the People of the South.* New York: Crown, 1949.

Cohen, Hennig, and William B. Dillingham, eds. *Humor in the Old Southwest.* Boston: Houghton, 1964.

Johnson, Clifton H., ed. *God Struck Me Dead: Religious Conversion Experiences and Autobiographies of Ex-slaves.* Philadelphia: Pilgrim Press, 1969.

Phillips, Ulrich B., ed. *Plantation and Frontier, 1649–1863.* 2 vols. 1910; rpt. New York: Burt Franklin, 1969.

Sprague, William B. *Annals of the American Pulpit: or Commemorative Notices of Distinguished American Clergymen of Various Denominations, from the Early Settlement of the Country to the Close of the Year Eighteen Hundred and Fifty-Five.* 9 vols. New York: Robert Carter and Bros. Vol. III: *Presbyterians,* 1858; vol. IV: *Presbyterians,* 1868; vol. VI: *Baptists,* 1860; vol. VII: *Methodists,* 1861.

Sweet, William Warren, ed. *Religion on the American Frontier. A*

Collection of Source Materials. 4 vols. Vol. I: *The Baptists, 1783–1830.* New York: Holt, 1931. Vol. II: *The Presbyterians, 1783–1840.* New York: Harper, 1936. Vol. III: *The Congregationalists, 1783–1850.* Chicago: Univ. of Chicago Press, 1939. Vol. IV: *The Methodists, 1783–1840.* Chicago: Univ. of Chicago Press, 1946.

Yetman, Norman R., ed. *Life under the "Peculiar Institution": Selections from the Slave Narrative Collection.* New York: Holt, 1970.

SECONDARY SOURCES

Books

Abernethy, Thomas Perkins. *The Formative Period in Alabama, 1815–1828.* Montgomery: Brown Printing Co., 1922.

———. *From Frontier to Plantation in Tennessee: A Study in Frontier Democracy.* Chapel Hill: Univ. of North Carolina Press, 1932.

———. *The South in the New Nation, 1789–1819.* Baton Rouge: Louisiana State Univ. Press, 1961.

———. *Three Virginia Frontiers.* Baton Rouge: Louisiana State Univ. Press, 1940.

Benson, Louis F. *The English Hymn: Its Development and Use in Worship.* 1915; rpt., Richmond: John Knox Press, 1962.

Billington, Ray Allen. *Westward Expansion: A History of the American Frontier.* New York: Macmillan, 1949.

Boles, John B. *The Great Revival, 1787–1805: The Origins of the Southern Evangelical Mind.* Lexington: Univ. Press of Kentucky, 1972.

Brandon, S. G. F. *The Judgment of the Dead: The Idea of Life after Death in the Major Religions.* New York: Scribner's, 1967.

Bridenbaugh, Carl. *Myths and Realities: Societies of the Colonial South.* Baton Rouge: Louisiana State Univ. Press, 1952.

Buck, Solon Justus. *Illinois in 1818.* 2nd ed., rev., Chicago: McClurg, 1918.

——— and Elizabeth Hawthorn Buck. *The Planting of Civilization in Western Pennsylvania.* Pittsburgh: Univ. of Pittsburgh Press, 1939.

Bucke, Emory Stevens, ed. *The History of American Methodism.* Nashville: Abingdon, 1964.

Cash, W. J. *The Mind of the South.* New York: Knopf, 1941.

Charles, R. H. *Eschatology: The Doctrine of a Future Life in Israel,*

Judaism and Christianity: A Critical History. 2nd ed., 1913; rpt. New York: Schocken, 1963.

Chase, Gilbert. *America's Music, from the Pilgrims to the Present.* 2nd rev. ed., New York: McGraw-Hill, 1966.

Chiles, Robert E. *Theological Transition in American Methodism, 1790–1935.* Nashville: Abingdon, 1965.

Clark, Blanche H. *The Tennessee Yeomen, 1840–1860.* Nashville: Vanderbilt Univ. Press, 1942.

Clark, Thomas D. *Frontier America: The Story of the Westward Movement.* New York: Scribner's, 1959.

Cleveland, Catharine C. *The Great Revival in the West, 1797–1805.* Chicago: Univ. of Chicago Press, 1916; rpt. Gloucester, Mass.: Peter Smith, 1959.

Cohn, Norman. *The Pursuit of the Millennium: Revolutionary Messianism in Medieval and Reformation Europe and Its Bearing on Modern Totalitarian Movements.* 2nd ed., New York: Harper, 1961.

Cross, Whitney R. *The Burned-over District: The Social and Intellectual History of Enthusiastic Religion in Western New York, 1800–1850.* New York: Harper, 1965.

Cullman, Oscar. *The Christology of the New Testament,* trans. Shirley C. Guthrie and Charles A. M. Hall. Philadelphia: Westminster, 1959.

Dick, Everett. *The Dixie Frontier: A Social History of the Southern Frontier from the First Transmontane Beginnings to the Civil War.* New York: Knopf, 1948; paper ed., Capricorn, 1964.

Dorson, Richard M. *American Folklore.* Chicago: Univ. of Chicago Press, 1959.

Drake, St. Clair, and Horace R. Cayton. *Black Metropolis: A Study of Negro Life in a Northern City.* 2 vols. New York: Harper, 1962.

Eaton, Clement. *The Growth of Southern Civilization, 1790–1860.* New York: Harper, 1963.

Eighmy, John Lee. *Churches in Cultural Captivity: A History of the Social Attitudes of Southern Baptists.* Knoxville: Univ. of Tennessee Press, 1972.

Eliade, Mircea. *Rites and Symbols of Initiation: The Mysteries of Birth and Rebirth,* trans. Willard R. Trask. New York: Harper, 1965.

Gennep, Arnold van. *The Rites of Passage,* trans. Monika B. Vizedom and Gabrielle L. Caffee. Chicago: Univ. of Chicago Press, 1960.

Genovese, Eugene D. *In Red and Black: Marxian Explorations in Southern and Afro-American History.* New York: Pantheon, 1971.

————. *The Political Economy of Slavery: Studies in the Economy and Society of the Slave South.* New York: Vintage, 1967.

Haller, William. *The Rise of Puritanism, or, The Way to the New Jerusalem as Set Forth in Pulpit and Press from Thomas Cartwright to John Liliburne and John Milton, 1570–1643.* New York: Columbia Univ. Press, 1938; paper ed., New York: Harper, 1957.

Hill, Samuel S., Jr. *Southern Churches in Crisis.* New York: Holt, 1967.

Hobsbawm, E. J. *Primitive Rebels: Studies in Archaic Forms of Social Movement in the 19th and 20th Centuries.* New York: Praeger, 1959; paper ed., New York: Norton, 1965.

Jackson, George Pullen. *Another Sheaf of White Spirituals.* Gainesville: Univ. of Florida Press, 1952.

————. *Down East Spirituals and Others: Three Hundred Songs Supplemental to the Author's Spiritual Folk-Songs of Early America.* New York: Augustin, 1939.

————. *Spiritual Folk-Songs of Early America: Two Hundred and Fifty Tunes and Texts with an Introduction and Notes.* New York: Augustin, 1937; rpt., New York: Dover, 1964.

————. *White and Negro Spirituals, Their Life Span and Kinship, Tracing 200 Years of Untrammeled Song Making and Singing Among Our Country Folk, with 116 Songs as Sung by Both Races.* New York: Augustin, 1943.

————. *White Spirituals in the Southern Uplands: The Story of the Fasola Folk, Their Songs, Singings, and "Buckwheat Notes."* Chapel Hill: Univ. of North Carolina Press, 1933; rpt., New York: Dover, 1965.

Johnson, Charles A. *The Frontier Camp Meeting: Religion's Harvest Time.* Dallas: Southern Methodist Univ. Press, 1955.

Johnson, Guion Griffis. *Ante-Bellum North Carolina: A Social History.* Chapel Hill: Univ. of North Carolina Press, 1937.

Kaplan, Louis, comp., in association with James Tyler Cook, Clinton E. Colby, Jr., and Daniel C. Haskell. *A Bibliography of American Autobiographies.* Madison: Univ. of Wisconsin Press, 1962.

Land, Aubrey C., ed. *Bases of the Plantation Society.* Columbia: Univ. of South Carolina Press, 1969.

Lazenby, Marion Elias. *History of Methodism in Alabama and West*

Florida: Being an Account of the Amazing March of Methodism through Alabama and West Florida. Nashville: n.p., 1960.

Lehmann, Theo. *Negro Spirituals: Geschichte und Theologie.* Berlin: Evangelische Verlagsanstalt, 1965.

Lewis, I. M. *Ecstatic Religion: An Anthropological Study of Spirit Possession and Shamanism.* Baltimore: Penguin, 1971.

Lomax, Alan. *Folk Song Style and Culture.* Washington, D. C.: American Association for the Advancement of Science, Pub. No. 88, 1968.

Mathews, Donald G. *Slavery and Methodism: A Chapter in American Morality, 1780–1845.* Princeton: Princeton Univ. Press, 1965.

Meyers, Marvin. *The Jacksonian Persuasion: Politics and Belief.* New York: Vintage, 1960.

Miyakawa, T. Scott. *Protestants and Pioneers: Individualism and Conformity on the American Frontier.* Chicago: Univ. of Chicago Press, 1964.

Moore, Albert Burton. *History of Alabama and Her People.* Chicago: American Historical Society, 1927.

Moore, Arthur K. *The Frontier Mind.* Lexington: Univ. of Kentucky Press, 1957; paper ed., New York: McGraw-Hill, 1963.

Morgan, Edmund S. *Visible Saints: The History of a Puritan Idea.* Ithaca: Cornell Univ. Press, 1965.

Nagler, Arthur Wilford. *Pietism and Methodism, or, The Significance of German Pietism in the Origin and Early Development of Methodism.* Nashville: Publishing House of the M. E. Church, South, 1918.

Niebuhr, H. Richard. *The Social Sources of Denominationalism.* Cleveland: World, 1957.

Ott, Philip Wesley. "The Mind of Early American Methodism: 1800–1844." Diss., Univ. of Pennsylvania, 1968.

Owsley, Frank Lawrence. *Plain Folk of the Old South.* Baton Rouge: Louisiana State Univ. Press, 1949; paper ed., Chicago: Quadrangle, 1965.

Philbrick, Francis S. *The Rise of the West, 1754–1830.* New York: Harper, 1966.

Phillips, Ulrich B. *Life and Labor in the Old South.* Boston: Little, 1929.

Pope, Liston. *Millhands and Preachers: A Study of Gastonia.* New Haven: Yale Univ. Press, 1942.

Posey, Walter Brownlow. *The Baptist Church in the Lower Missis-*

sippi Valley, 1776–1845. Lexington: Univ. of Kentucky Press, 1957.

————. *The Development of Methodism in the Old Southwest, 1783–1824.* Tuscaloosa, Ala.: Weatherford Printing, 1933.

————. *Frontier Mission: A History of Religion West of the Southern Appalachians to 1861.* Lexington: Univ. of Kentucky Press, 1966.

————. *The Presbyterian Church in the Old Southwest, 1778–1838.* Richmond: John Knox Press, 1952.

Riley, B. F. *History of the Baptists of Alabama: From the Time of Their First Occupation of Alabama in 1808, until 1894.* Birmingham: Roberts and Son, 1895.

Rosen, George. *Madness in Society: Chapters in the Historical Sociology of Mental Illness.* Chicago: Univ. of Chicago Press, 1968.

Rourke, Constance. *American Humor: A Study of the National Character.* New York: Harcourt, 1931; paper ed., Garden City, N.Y.: Anchor, 1953.

Scott, Anne Firor. *The Southern Lady: From Pedestal to Politics, 1830–1930.* Chicago: Univ. of Chicago Press, 1970.

Sellers, Charles Coleman. *Lorenzo Dow: The Bearer of the Word.* New York: Minton, Balch, 1928.

Shea, Daniel B. *Spiritual Autobiography in Early America.* Princeton: Princeton Univ. Press, 1968.

Sweet, William Warren. *Religion in the Development of American Culture, 1765–1840.* New York: Scribner's, 1952.

————. *The Story of Religion in America.* Rev. and enlarged ed., New York: Harper, 1950.

Sydnor, Charles S. *The Development of Southern Sectionalism, 1819–1848.* Baton Rouge: Louisiana State Univ. Press, 1948.

Takaki, Ronald T. *A Pro-Slavery Crusade: The Agitation to Reopen the African Slave Trade.* New York: Free Press, 1971.

Taylor, Rosser Howard. *Ante-Bellum South Carolina: A Social and Cultural History.* Chapel Hill: Univ. of North Carolina Press, 1942; rpt., New York: Da Capo Press, 1970.

Turner, Victor W. *The Ritual Process: Structure and Anti-Structure.* Chicago: Aldine, 1969.

United States Dept. of Commerce, Bureau of the Census. *Negro Population, 1790–1915.* Washington, D. C.: Government Printing Office, 1918; rpt., New York: Arno Press and the *New York Times,* 1968.

————. *The Statistical History of the United States from Colonial Times to the Present.* Stamford, Conn.: Fairfield, 1965.

Vance, Rupert B. *Human Factors in Cotton Culture: A Study in the Social Geography of the American South.* Chapel Hill: Univ. of North Carolina Press, 1929.

————. *Human Geography of the South: A Study in Regional Resources and Human Adequacy.* Chapel Hill: Univ. of North Carolina Press, 1932.

Wallace, Anthony F. C. *Religion: An Anthropological View.* New York: Random House, 1966.

Ward, John William. *Andrew Jackson—Symbol for an Age.* New York: Oxford Univ. Press, 1962.

Wertenbaker, Thomas Jefferson. *The Old South: The Founding of American Civilization.* New York: Scribner's, 1942; rpt., New York: Cooper Square, 1963.

Wiley, Bell Irvin. *The Plain People of the Confederacy.* Baton Rouge: Louisiana State Univ. Press, 1944; paper ed., Chicago: Quadrangle, 1963.

Woodman, Harold D., ed. *Slavery and the Southern Economy: Sources and Readings.* New York: Harcourt, 1966.

Yoder, Don. *Pennsylvania Spirituals.* Lancaster: Pennsylvania Folklife Society, 1961.

Essays and Articles

Boatright, Mody C. "The Myth of Frontier Individualism," in *Turner and the Sociology of the Frontier,* ed. Richard Hofstadter and Seymour Martin Lipset, 43–64. New York: Basic Books, 1968.

Brauer, Jerald C. "Changing Perspectives on Religion in America," in *Reinterpretation in American Church History.* Chicago: Univ. of Chicago Press, 1968.

Brewer, Earl D. C. "Sect and Church in Methodism," *Social Forces* 30 (1951–52), 400–8.

Brown, Richard Maxwell, "The American Vigilante Tradition," in *Violence in America: Historical and Comparative Perspectives,* ed. Hugh Davis Graham and Ted Robert Gurr, 154–226. New York: Bantam, 1969.

Buck, Paul H. "The Poor Whites of the Ante-Bellum South," *American Historical Review* 31 (1925), 41–54.

Bibliography

Cabaniss, Francis A., and James A. Cabaniss. "Religion in Ante-Bellum Mississippi," *Journal of Mississippi History* 6 (1944), 191–224.

Crutchfield, Mary Elizabeth. "The White Spiritual." Thesis, Union Theological Seminary, 1946.

Eaton, Clement. "Class Differences in the Old South," *Virginia Quarterly Review* 33 (1957), 357–70.

Ellinwood, Leonard. "Religious Music in America," in *Religious Perspectives in American Culture* (*Religion in American Life*, vol. II), ed. James Ward Smith and A. Leland Jamison, 289–359. Princeton: Princeton Univ. Press, 1961.

Fernandez, James W. "Symbolic Consensus in a Fang Reformative Cult," *American Anthropologist* 67 (1965), 902–29.

Frantz, Joe B. "The Frontier Tradition: An Invitation to Violence," in *Violence in America*, ed. Graham and Gurr, 127–54.

Geertz, Clifford. "Religion as a Cultural System," in *The Interpretation of Cultures: Selected Essays*, 87–125. New York: Basic Books, 1973.

Hamilton, W. B. "Mississippi in 1817: A Sociological and Economic Analysis," *Journal of Mississippi History* 24 (1967), 270–92.

Horton, Robin. "African Conversion," *Africa* 41 (1971), 85–108.

————. "The Kalibari World View: An Outline and Interpretation," *Africa* 32 (1962), 197–220.

Hymes, Dell. "Some North Pacific Coast Poems: A Problem in Anthropological Philology," *American Anthropologist* 67 (1965), 316–41.

Jackson, George Pullen. "Buckwheat Notes," *The Musical Quarterly* 19 (1933), 393–400.

Johnson, Charles A. "The Frontier Camp-Meeting: Contemporary and Historical Appraisals," *Mississippi Valley Historical Review* 37 (1950–51), 91–110.

Linden, Fabian. "Economic Democracy in the Slave South: An Appraisal of Some Recent Views," *Journal of Negro History* 31 (1946), 140–89.

Lowery, Charles D. "The Great Migration to the Mississippi Territory, 1789–1819," *Journal of Mississippi History* 30 (1968), 173–92.

Lynch, William O. "The Westward Flow of Southern Colonists Before 1861," *Journal of Southern History* 9 (1943), 303–27.

Murphey, Murray G. "On the Relation between Science and Religion," *American Quarterly* 20 (1968), 275–95.

Phillips, Ulrich B. "The Origin and Growth of the Southern Black Belts," *American Historical Review* 11 (1906), 798–816.

Rothstein, Morton. "The Antebellum South as a Dual Economy: A Tentative Hypothesis," *Agricultural History* 41 (1967), 373–82.

Russel, Robert R. "The Effects of Slavery Upon Nonslaveholders in the Ante Bellum South," *Agricultural History* 15 (1941), 112–26.

Tilly, Charles. "Collective Violence in European Perspective," in *Violence in America*, ed. Graham and Gurr, 4–45.

Turner, Victor W. "Betwixt and Between: The Liminal Period in *Rites de Passage*," in *Symposium on New Approaches in the Study of Religion*, Proceedings of the American Ethnological Society, 1964, ed. June Helm, 4–20. Seattle: Univ. of Washington Press, 1964.

INDEXES

First Lines of Hymns and Choruses

(Lines in brackets not quoted directly in text)

GENERAL INDEX

Index

Reed, Andrew, and James Matheson: quoted, 78, 101
Religion: role in Southern society, 4, 45–46; concept in choruses, 119–20
Richardson, Wade Hampton, 23; quoted, 23–24
Role reversal, in camp-meeting, 76, 86–87, 132–33

Sacred Harp (tune book), 93
Santayana, George: quoted, 134
Satan, role in camp-meeting, 79
Scotch-Irish: in settlement of South, 14, 36
Sermons, 74, 75, 81, 88–89
Sinners, role in camp-meeting, 77
Slavery: relation to plain-folk, 18–19, 22, 23–24, 25; churches' attitudes toward, 57–58
Social mobility in South, 19, 123, 128–29
South Carolina, 16, 93
Southern Harmony, The (tune book), 92, 93
Spiritual choruses: as plain-folk exegesis, 10–11, 93–95, 96, 97, 121–22; origins and development, 90–91
Spiritual singing, in camp-meeting, 80, 85, 89, 91, 97, 127
Spiritual verses, 90, 122 n.63
Stennett, Samuel, 90
Stewardship: plain-folk conception, 119
Stone, Barton W., 52
Storm: spiritual image, 99, 100, 117
Stranger: spiritual image, 99, 102
Sturdivant, Matthew P., 45

Supplement to the Kentucky Harmony, A (tune book), 92
Swayze, William: quoted, 83

Tennessee, 14, 15, 19, 24, 36, 44, 45, 52, 82, 83
Testimonials, 76, 81, 89
Tevis, John: quoted, 82–83
Texas, 14, 17, 28
Thomas à Kempis, 8
Transylvania Seminary, 36–37
Trollope, Mrs. Frances: quoted, 78, 82
Tune books, 91–92; compilers, 91–93

Vardeman, Jeremiah, 63, 64
Vigilantism, 31
Virginia, 18, 24, 32, 38, 44, 63, 92, 101, 103

Walker, William ("Singin' Billy"), 92–93
Watts, Isaac, 90
Weld, Isaac: quoted, 33
Wesley, Charles, 90
Wesley, John, 8, 39, 41, 57, 109, 119; quoted, 101
Western Christian Monitor, 83
White, Benjamin Franklin, 93
Women: in plain-folk society, 27–28, 64; in camp-meeting, 76, 79, 86–87, 132
World-rejection: in plain-folk religion, 98–99, 102, 106, 125–26, 129

Young, Jacob, 43–44, 67; quoted, 44, 66, 121

Zuber, William Physick, 17

And They All Sang Hallelujah was manually set on the Linotype in eleven-point Garamond No. 3 with one-point line spacing. Fry's Ornamented foundry type was selected for display on the title page and for chapter opening set-ins.

The book was designed by Jim Billingsley, composed and printed letterpress by Heritage Printers, Inc., Charlotte, North Carolina, and bound by Carolina Ruling and Binding Company, also of Charlotte.

The paper on which the book is printed is designed for an effective life of at least three hundred years.

THE UNIVERSITY OF TENNESSEE PRESS
KNOXVILLE